The Experience of Retirement

The Experience of Retirement

Robert S. Weiss

With a Foreword by David J. Ekerdt

ILR Press
an imprint of Cornell University Press
Ithaca and London

First published 2005 by Cornell University Press
First printing, Cornell Paperbacks, 2005

Printed in the United States of America

Library of Congress Cataloging-in-Publication Data

Weiss, Robert Stuart, 1925–
    The experience of retirement / Robert S. Weiss ; with a foreword by David J. Ekerdt.
        p. cm.
    Includes bibliographical references and index.
    ISBN-13: 978-0-8014-4406-7 (cloth : alk. paper)
    ISBN-10: 0-8014-4406-3 (cloth : alk. paper)
    ISBN-13: 978-0-8014-7252-7 (pbk. : alk. paper)
    ISBN-10: 0-8014-7252-0 (pbk. : alk. paper)
    1. Retirement—United States.   2. Retirees—United States.   I. Title.
    HQ1063.2.U6W45 2005
    306.3'8'0973—dc22

                                    2005017716

Cornell University Press strives to use environmentally responsible suppliers and materials to the fullest extent possible in the publishing of its books. Such materials include vegetable-based, low-VOC inks and acid-free papers that are recycled, totally chlorine-free, or partly composed of non-wood fibers. For further information, visit our website at www.cornellpress.cornell.edu.

Cloth printing   10 9 8 7 6 5 4 3 2 1
Paperback printing   10 9 8 7 6 5 4 3 2 1

For Joan

Contents

Foreword
David J. Ekerdt

Ever since I learned that Robert Weiss was writing this book, I have been waiting for it, and for three reasons. First, this volume gives us what we do not have enough of: good descriptive studies of the experience of retirement. There is an enormous trade in practical advice about personal finances and planning for retirement. Scholars turn out policy analyses about the older worker, pensions, and income security, along with survey-based reports about all phases of the retirement process. However, we can count on one hand the books that make vivid what it feels like to become retired, explore the things that lead people to consider leaving their work careers and how they live with their decisions, document how money and marriage affect the quality of life, and suggest what can be gained from different ways of organizing life in retirement.

My second reason for anticipating this book is that it comes from Robert Weiss, someone who has made a career of observing and listening to people as they respond to new life situations. His previous books have accompanied men and women through such circumstances as marital separation, single parenting, bereavement, and the stresses of work at midlife. "Learning from strangers" (as he once described his approach), Weiss has attended to adults trying to make sense of the doors that are opening and closing in their lives. In this new work on retirement, the learning from others may have been even more careful and empathetic because Weiss is himself of retirement age.

To recognize what is unique about Robert Weiss' observations on retirement, consider some information that I gleaned from the Health and Retirement Study, an ongoing survey of more than 10,000 men and women in the United States who are in their 50s and 60s. Every two years this nationally representative panel is asked numerous questions about the progress of their lives, including (when it is timely) their reasons for and reactions to retirement. One such question asks, "Would you say that your retirement has turned out to be very satisfying, moderately satisfying, or not at all satisfying?" I compiled responses from nearly 3,500 participants aged 62 to 67 who said (in 1996, 1998, or 2000) that they were completely retired. As for how retirement has turned out, 62 percent said it was very satisfying, 30 percent said moderately satisfying, and 8 percent said it was not satisfying at all. Figures for men and women were virtually identical.

What can we learn from such replies? Well, a lot. The percentage distributions tell us that retired workers in general have a pretty positive opinion about life in retirement although a small minority find it to be disappointing. The results also tell us that the opinions of men and women line up the same way. With further analytic effort, the responses to these and other survey items can be compared among groups to determine whether opinion varies, for example, by age of retirement, by wealth or health, by marital situation, or by occupation. Circumstances can be combined into scenarios that project the retirements that are the most or least gratifying, comfortable, or financially secure. All this breadth of population coverage and numerical power can generate sweeping conclusions about contemporary retirement.

What we do not learn from such research is what people would say outside of the limited, one-shot response alternatives that the survey format requires. Would they shade or qualify their views about retired life, equivocate, or backtrack on something said earlier in the same conversation? Would they discuss the way their perspective has changed over time? Would they describe experiences unanticipated by the investigators?

To understand "what actual retirements are actually like," Robert Weiss and his colleagues held those longer and repeated conversations with eighty-nine women and men as they passed—some unevenly—

from work to retirement. What the Weiss project brings us is information, yes, but also something equally valuable: people in the act of interpreting their own experience at a new life stage. Responses from surveys are akin to the knowledge one gets by observing geographic features from an airplane at 30,000 feet. What we see is valid and useful but not the same as the impressions we would gain from a journey across the surface. It is at this different, closer scale that Weiss invites us to understand what it is like to retire.

From the outset, the open-ended nature of retirement is apparent when trying to define it. The line between working and retired is not always clear, and the author himself is not completely sure about his own retirement situation. As to why people retire, Weiss can assign people to categories (e.g., want leisure, health reasons, job troubles), but he also presents the case of Mr. Mathers who gives, by my count, four separate reasons for having retired, one opening into the other and all irreducible to a single decision.

One of the clearest themes from these conversations is the ambivalence of retired life, how "retirement is apt to be a mixed experience." Weiss finds people saying this in many ways. They contemplate retirement with hope and apprehension, want leisure but are still invested in work, and cherish the absence of stress and responsibility but miss the opportunity for achievement. Retirees have the sweet freedom of nothing special to do, but having nothing special to do likewise makes one socially marginal. Relief from the interpersonal obligations of the workplace also means fewer people with whom to exchange favors or information. With grandchildren, retirees want both affection and autonomy—wary of being pressed into service for child care but glad to be needed. Financially comfortable retirees still admit anxiety about the long term. The experience of retirement, as told here, can be bittersweet. Commenting on this, Weiss observes that not every retiree reports gains and losses to the same degree, but "most will have some familiarity with them all."

My third reason for looking forward to this book is that I, too, face retirement. Once one relinquishes engagement in work and the responsibility of parenting, one has great freedom, yes, but freedom for what? The new retirees in this study were feeling their way toward understanding how and to whom they now mattered, working it out in their minds: This is who I am now, this is how I structure my days, these are the people with whom I belong, this is how I see the future.

Having listened with unusual attention to the way in which these women and men make meaning of their passage, Weiss concludes with a chapter of advice to prospective retirees about money, planning, leave-taking from work, relationships, relocation, and the use of time. I will recommend this book to others, and if I sense that they will not read it through right away, I will urge them to at least consult the last chapter. It distills the essence well. For all of us wondering whether to embrace or resist our retired future selves, Weiss does not tell us what it is we should do but does give us the understandings we will inevitably need.

The Experience of Retirement

Introduction

What Does It Mean to Be Retired?

Defining retirement can be surprisingly difficult. There are, in general, three approaches. I call them the economic, the psychological, and the sociological.

The economic approach assumes that a person older than his or her mid-fifties is retired if he or she does not work, or at least does not work for money.[1] Bills are paid by a pension or Social Security or withdrawals from savings or investments. This approach assumes that the person does not desire to work; otherwise, he or she would just be unemployed. A younger person who did not have work and did not want to work probably would not fit the underlying idea of the economic definition. Such a person might be thought of as rich and lucky or poor and shiftless but probably not as retired—unless he or she was a former athlete.

The economic approach to defining retirement also tends to be less clear-cut in regard to people who have retired from their careers but have substantial part-time employment. Adherents of such an approach may say that such people are only partially retired, but then the question arises of just how much work is necessary before a retirement is a partial retirement. The economic approach may also falter when it encounters older people without paid work who would gladly accept work if only they could get it. Adherents of the economic approach then have to decide whether to classify such people as retired despite themselves.

The second approach, the psychological, asks whether the person has established a retirement identity. According to this approach, you are retired if you think you are. Being retired means that you say of yourself that you are a former manager or former bookkeeper or former professor or former whatever, but now you are retired.[2] This is the definition of retirement used by survey studies of retirement.

The only problem of classification that the psychological approach is likely to encounter occurs when people themselves are not sure whether they are retired, as when they have retired from what had been their careers but now work at something new. Also, self-definitions can change abruptly as people change their sense of themselves as being in or out of the labor force. A former owner of a construction company whom we came to know had signed over his company to his two children, at which point he defined himself as retired. But after several months of worrying that the children were not doing well with an important project, he returned to resume direction of the company. He did not go on the payroll, and so his economic situation did not change, but his definition of himself did.

Finally, there is the sociological definition of retirement. According to this approach, you are retired if you have left your career and occupy a social niche in which it is socially acceptable to be without work. In this approach you are retired if others see you as retired.

This is the definition of retirement that I think we use in everyday life. And yet it may be the least clear-cut of the definitions: it requires others' ratification, and there is no specific point at which this can assuredly be obtained. A retiree to whom I refer later in the book had been without steady employment for years, although he had once been a successful lawyer. He said he was delighted to reach his mid-sixties because he could then tell others that he was retired. Not until then could he be sure his claim to retirement status would be accepted.

By and large, people who are retired by one definition are also retired by the others. But inconsistencies can occur. People who retire from the military can be too young to be thought of as seniors and may, in consequence, wonder whether they are legitimately retired or are rather between occupations. Self-employed consultants, agents, accountants, and writers can see no need ever to say that they have retired despite their hours of work having dropped toward zero. I know a financial counselor in his nineties who has retained a very few clients. His son says he has retired, but he does not.

As I write this, I myself am of retirement age. Some fourteen years ago I formally retired from a teaching position. I arranged to receive the pension to which I had contributed over the years, and became an emeritus in my former department. With my income now provided primarily by the pension and by Social Security, the economic definition of retirement would unhesitatingly classify me as retired.

Yet I continue to work as a sociologist—for which statement I offer this book as evidence. To be sure, I no longer have research funds, no longer head a research group, and no longer fret about meeting deadlines for progress reports. I work at my own pace. I am pretty sure I work less than I did when I was in mid-career, and without question I work less efficiently. Because I do not have classes to meet, I spend more time with the morning newspaper, which is something one does when one is retired. But as far as the psychological definition of retirement goes, I am resistive. I do not want to think of myself as retired.

Yet it is evident to me that my approach to my work has changed. Now and then I go through files that contain correspondence and papers and notes from my earlier years in the field, with the idea of discarding what I do not need (which is pretty much everything). As I do this, I am jolted by the recognition of how active I once was. I met classes, attended conferences, developed research proposals, conducted research, served on review boards, and maintained a number of collaborations. The social niche I now occupy is much quieter.

I still have an office at my university, but I am there only irregularly. And it is the smallest office I have occupied since leaving my graduate student cubicle. I still am in touch with students, but increasingly what I do for them is limited to providing letters of reference. Sometimes I get asked to lecture or to lead a workshop or to participate in a panel, and I am pleased when that happens, but it does not happen nearly as often as it once did. When I attend a professional conference, as I do occasionally, I tend to feel marginal to its proceedings and regularly am startled by how far the field has come since I last checked. At a conference a couple of years ago, I met a young person who had read something I had written three or four decades earlier who said, as best I can recall, that she felt honored to meet me and had thought I was dead.

I have not carried a teaching load in years, and do not want to tie myself down that way again. When I take on a small research project, as I have a couple of times recently, I have the feeling that I have chosen to use some of my free time for the project, just as I might have chosen to use it for an active vacation. I suspect that sociologically I am retired.

I find my present status both gratifying and frustrating. It is gratifying in its freedom, in enabling me to choose how I spend my time. It is frustrating when I regret that I am not a more active participant in what has been my occupational community. But in truth nothing prevents me from doing as much as I can. And I still do participate at some level in the community of sociologists. On the other hand, that community does seem increasingly to be staffed by decidedly younger people.

I find retirement perplexing, even as I write about it. The freedom to do anything includes the freedom to remain engaged as well as the freedom to do nothing. And yet there is something special about the style in which I, as well as former colleagues who are now retired, remain engaged, to the extent that we do. Whatever our ultimate goals—to leave a legacy, to complete a life's work, to contribute to our society, to keep busy—we are not trying to establish ourselves in our careers. That is done, over.

My relationship to time puzzles me. I am able, within limits, to take whatever time I need to do whatever I want to do. And yet I feel pressed by time because I am aware that there is not so much of it left to me. Somewhere in the back of my mind I know that there is a closing bell and that I am getting nearer to when it will sound. Yet there is no urgency except as I impose it. All in all, I suppose I am retired, by any definition.

Actually, I did not begin the study of retirement that I report on here because I was perplexed by my own retirement. The perplexity came later, as I tried to put myself in the context of retirees. The study of retirement in general began as a logical continuation of an earlier study I had done on work as experienced by occupationally successful men, and led to the question of how the men would react to work's absence when they retired.

This earlier study continued still earlier research. Even as a sociologist one specializes, and the problems I have worked on in my career have had to do with social relationships: what they provide and what happens when they are lost or absent. In the 1960s I began a series of studies of marriage and other pair bonds, focusing on the consequences of their loss or absence. I then became interested in the way people put relationships together to provide a satisfactory way of life and to deal with its everyday stresses. With this in mind I studied the ways in which occupationally successful men dealt with the sometimes competing, sometimes mutually sustaining, relationships of work and family.[3]

What I found in that study was that although their families mattered much more to the men than their work did—assuring their families' well-being was their ultimate commitment—the men felt that success at work was necessary if they were to meet what they believed to be their familial responsibilities. Success at work enabled them to provide their families with what they understood them to need, which included not only a good-enough standard of living but also a good-enough place in their communities.[4] Doing well on the job made it possible for them to be the husbands and fathers they wanted to be.

Yet this was only part of the explanation for their engagement with work. Their work gave them not only interesting, challenging tasks to perform but also almost constant opportunity for interchange with others. There were meetings to attend and people to check with and brief conversations in hallways. Those who worked in organizations formed partnerships and alliances and entered into competitions. They could become members of teams striving after shared goals. They could be recognized for achievements. They might find themselves caught up in dramas in which rivalries were acted out and from which winners and losers emerged. Simply belonging mattered: just being a member of the community of work could help sustain their identities and feelings of worth.

My question was, given the many provisions of work, how would men and women respond to retirement and, with it, the loss of their occupation and their membership in its community? Although the study's subjects had been men, I could not see why work should matter less to women. And so I wanted to know, for both men and women, whether the emotional and social provisions of their work could be found in other relationships and, if they could not, what would be the consequences. One possibility was that the ending of work would leave a persisting deficit in life. Another was that retirees would be so relieved to be done with work's stresses, and so pleased by retirement's freedom, that they would not mind retirement a bit. But fundamentally, we did not know.

The value of retirement was something only retirees could judge. It seemed important to interview a sample of retirees about the way that retirement had changed not only their daily activities but the quality of their lives.

From the beginning I had coworkers who helped me think through the kind of sample we would need and how to recruit the members of the sample and what sort of information we would need from them.[5] Our aim was to capture the experiences of retiring and adapting to retirement and to describe how those experiences came about. We decided to interview people who were likely to have retired from careers rather than from the last in a succession of unrelated jobs, and that suggested that our sample should be more or less middle class. We had in mind people whose work had been administrative, managerial, professional, or academic.

We wanted to learn about the minutia of retirement: how the day was spent, what was involved in voluntary activity. We would, therefore, have to conduct interviews in which we gave respondents adequate time to develop accounts of how things happened, to recall conversations, and to describe their present and past feelings and thoughts. It also seemed important to interview people more than once: to interview them before their retirement, when they were thinking about an impending retirement; then again just after their retirement, when they could describe its meanings; then a year or two later, when they could report on how it was working out.

Interviews like those we were planning produce a lot of information. An interview that goes an hour and a half can produce a transcript of about forty single-spaced pages. Given our hope of obtaining three interviews with each respondent, we would have to limit the number of respondents. Our experience in other studies suggested that approximately ninety to a hundred respondents would be as large a sample as we could manage comfortably without resorting to quantitative summaries that would lose the texture of the data.

We wanted to interview people who had pursued a range of middle-class careers. We thought we would find an adequate range of experiences within a sample of thirty men and thirty women, but trying for a larger sample still seemed to be a good idea. We had to anticipate attrition, as respondents moved away between a first and second interview or just decided after a first interview that they did not want to participate in a second one. Taking everything together, it seemed prudent to try for ninety respondents, with the proviso that the sample include a minimum of thirty men and thirty women.

My colleagues and I looked to the Boston suburbs for our sample. We chose six suburbs that were by repute middle class, although one, as it turned out, would have been better described as upper middle class, and one a combination of middle class and not-so-middle class. The Commonwealth of Massachusetts requires that every municipality publish a voters list containing the names, ages, and occupations of everyone at every address. This provided us with lists from which to choose potential respondents. We randomly selected people in each of our suburbs who were sixty or older and were listed as still working. We sent them a letter explaining the study, then called them to ask if they had plans to retire. If they said that they did, or if they said they had retired just recently, we asked if we could come talk with them.

Our first pass at sampling did not turn up quite enough employed women of retirement age. I mentioned this to a journalist friend who wrote a column on aging for a local newspaper. The friend noted our study in her column and also noted that there were not that many women in the voters list whose ages and occupations made them appropriate for our study. After her column appeared, we received a half-dozen offers from women retiring from managerial and professional occupations who volunteered to take part in our study. We accepted the offers, with the result that our sample of retired women includes six women who were self-selected. We also accepted three men referred to the study by personnel managers for local firms with whom we had talked before deciding to rely on a community sample.[6] So our sample is basically a community sample, but not entirely.

We had not initially expected that people who had firm plans to retire would change their minds, but that happened with three respondents with whom we had held preretirement interviews. One was a
human relations officer who had been convinced by his coworkers that
they could not manage without him; another was a seventy-year-old
owner of a small business who never found anyone to buy him out;
the third was an accountant, aged sixty-two, who decided to work a
few more years to make sure that his retirement income would be
adequate.

We scheduled our interviews at intervals of about a year. In only
about half the cases were we successful in having a first interview before our respondent's retirement. With the other half our first interviews were within a few months of retirements that had already
happened. We also lost fourteen respondents who had provided preretirement interviews, mostly because they left the area after their
retirement.

Several times we collected data in addition to the data we initially
planned to collect. We conducted four interviews over a period of three
years with a former editor who was having difficulty adapting to retirement and also with a former academic who entered an assisted living facility. We also included in our sample a couple of respondents
whose occupations were not middle class, although they lived in one
of our middle-class communities. One was a retired college janitor, the
other a former tool-and-die worker. In the process of locating respondents, we came across a couple who had planned to retire and then,
after a business reversal, found that they could not afford it, and we
conducted interviews with them.

We ended with eighty-nine respondents, not counting the couple
who could not afford to retire. Fifty-six of our respondents were men
and thirty-three women. (See tables 1 and 2 at the end of this introduction.) Most were interviewed at least twice after their retirement,
whether or not they had been interviewed before their retirement.

We tape-recorded our interviews and had the tapes transcribed
as computer files. In the book I quote extensively from those transcripts. I hope the quotations will convey the lived experience of our
respondents.

In my summaries of what we were told and in my choice of quotations I have done my utmost to play fair. I have presented lengthy quotations from respondents whose experiences seemed to me to illustrate a general phenomenon: for example, the vulnerability of some retirees to social isolation. But I have tried also to report on respondents whose experiences did not fit the norm and to provide at least brief quotations that would illustrate their different experiences.

Retirement and Its Images

The way people think about retirement has changed over the years, and properly so. For over a hundred years people have been retiring earlier and, to the extent that we have records, have had more healthy years in their retirement.

At the turn of the last century more than 60 percent of men sixty-five or older were in the labor force. By 1950 that percentage had dropped to around 40 percent. In the year 2002 the percentage had dropped to 17 percent.[7] Historical statistics on the retirement of women are hard to come by, but may be assumed to parallel those for men. In 2002, among women over the age of sixty-five, only about 10 percent were in the labor force.[8]

The low level of labor force participation beyond the age of sixty-five, among both men and women, suggests the extent to which retirement has become a normal phase of life. Comparisons of statistics for the year 2002 with those for the years 1992 and earlier indicate that the average age of retirement reached the bottom of its long decline in the late eighties and has since begun slowly to rise.[9] Nevertheless, the institution of retirement is firmly established and seems likely to remain so.

Statistics about the retirement ages of the population as a whole obscure the sizable differences among occupations. Members of the armed forces retire very early, sometimes in their forties. Police and firefighters commonly retire in their fifties. On the other hand, physicians retire very late, often in their seventies, and Supreme Court justices keep going into their eighties and beyond. But despite this occupational variation, sixty-five has been established in our thinking as a normal retirement age: retiring much before sixty-five is likely to be seen as an early retirement and much after it as a late retirement.

Retirees can expect a good many years of life in retirement. Life expectancy at age sixty-five is about sixteen years for men, about nineteen years for women.[10] Most of the years will be healthy: at age sixty-five men can expect about eleven years of freedom from physical, mental, or social impairment, women about fourteen.[11] These statistics are based on a general population and include people who already had health problems when they reached sixty-five. People who reach sixty-five without health problems can expect still more years free of impairment.

As retirement has increasingly become an expected phase of life, and one in which people remain healthy and active, the image of retirement has changed. The political cartoons of sixty and seventy years ago pictured the retired as having been worn out by work and age and, in consequence, having become marginal members of the community: put out to pasture; on the shelf; on the scrap heap. Those critical of industry argued that the retired were callously cast off by an industrial world that wanted youthful strength and energy. Some observers thought such casting off to be a good thing. William Graebner, in his history of retirement, notes that "William Ostler, a professor of medicine at Johns Hopkins, argued in 1905 that all men should retire at age 60 because by then they had lost all mental elasticity."[12]

In this older understanding of retirement, the retired were men without occupation, no longer of social value. Their lives were emotionally impoverished. T. S. Eliot wrote: "I have gone at dusk through narrow streets and watched the smoke that rises from the pipes of lonely men in shirtsleeves leaning out of windows." Many imagined that retirement hastened death. After the end of one's work, what else was left?

Current images of retirement could not be more different. In current images retirement is seen not as a reluctant acceptance of incapacity but rather as a desired release from obligation. Vitality remains, and now there is freedom to do with it whatever one wishes. In this spirit, an advertisement for a retirement village might present a robust man with iron gray hair and his equally attractive late-fifties wife, the two relaxed on a slope overlooking a golf course, content in their good health and their companionship. Money, the ad would suggest, would not be a problem, and it would be easy to believe that when they returned to their comfortable home they would have waiting for them a full calendar of social activities.[13]

Other current images of retirement also suggest an active, realized life. Retirement can be an opportunity for a second career, for becoming a lay minister or the owner of a franchised print shop or a computer consultant. It can permit adventure, travel, or a new way of life in another country. It can be a chance to realize dreams of artistic achievement, of creative enterprise as a painter or poet or musician or craftsman—dreams that had been put aside during the years of work. Or it can be a time for service, for contributing to programs that benefit others, as exemplified by Jimmy Carter's postpresidential involvement in world affairs.

Today's positive gloss on retirement extends even to those who prefer a less active retirement. Life in retirement can be seen as permitting a serene withdrawal from the stresses of preretirement life. The retired who choose a quiet life, far from being among society's discards, can be thought of as surrounded by the love of family and friends and happy to garden and to look after grandchildren.

These newer images of retirement are based on the important assumption that retirements are now well enough funded, at least for people who had middle-class careers, so that their earlier standard of living can be maintained. And, indeed, in the past few decades most retirees have been able to maintain their earlier standard of living. For those who now retire from government service or from academia, this is likely to continue to be the case. It is also likely to be the case for those who have enough in savings or investments.

Others may have to modify assumptions of a well-funded retirement at age sixty-five. Pension plans provided by the companies for which they work may no longer guarantee a particular payout. The Social Security Administration is gradually raising what it considers to be the "full retirement age" (with no reduction in benefits) to sixty-seven. Most troubling may be that retirees' costs for health care will rise because of more limited coverage by pension plans and Medicare, increased cost of insurance, increased co-payments, and increased likelihood that some costs can be covered only by retirees themselves.[14] In response to these developments, some will choose to stay at work longer than they otherwise would.

People typically go into retirement uncertain of how well their finances will hold up. Even so, they are generally better able to anticipate their retirement incomes than their retirement lives.[15] Programs intended to prepare people for retirement do not always help. Many of the programs concern themselves almost solely with financial matters: how much money will be needed and how it should be managed. And those that do not focus on finances tend to offer generalities: stay active, exercise, join groups.

One of our respondents, a woman we call Mrs. Hurst,* might be considered an example of someone who was worried about life in retirement. Mrs. Hurst was sixty-six and widowed. She had had a distinguished career in the field of social services. When we talked with her before her retirement, she was uncertain about retiring as director of an agency. Here is what she said:

I think this is the most difficult decision that I've come across. I've had some tough ones before, in terms of my children and a lot of other things. But this is really the toughest that I've encountered. Maybe my concerns are ridiculous and inordinate, all of that, but I don't know. I question, do you want to take some time not to have all of those pressures and responsibilities? Or do you really want to die with your boots on? And I don't know the answer to that. I have friends who have retired who have said they've never been so busy in their lives, that they're filling their lives with gratification. Which is very nice to hear. Knowing myself, I really would be very unhappy not having some motivation to get up and out of bed for—even if it's only a job that is routine and not very exciting. That's where I'm hung, really.

When we talked with Mrs. Hurst a year after her retirement, she described her first year in retirement as having been a mixed experience. She saw much more of her friends than she had when she was preoccupied by work. But she missed the engagement with others that

---

* All names of respondents have been changed. Other characteristics that could identify the respondents have been dropped or modified.

her job had provided. A few months after her retirement, she had suffered a bout of depression; a male friend had died, and that might have triggered it. Just recently she had signed up for a college course. She was currently looking for part-time work.

Mrs. Hurst's was only one experience of retirement. One person's retirement can be quite different from another's. And there were ways in which Mrs. Hurst's situation made for a more problematic retirement.

There is a large literature examining what might make for a better or less good retirement.[16] The married tend to do better than the unmarried, and Mrs. Hurst's retirement may have been made more difficult by her widowhood. In general, retirees who live alone are more vulnerable to social isolation. Also, although this was not an issue for Mrs. Hurst, financial problems are more likely to afflict women on their own than others.

Occupation makes a difference in the attractiveness of retirement.[17] Some occupations, such as police work, can be stressful enough to make those who pursue them think that retirement cannot come soon enough, although to the extent that membership in the police cuts one off from others, retirement may bring with it social isolation. Some occupations, including many academic fields, may be so interesting to those who pursue them that they want to put off retirement indefinitely; other occupations, like that of physicians, may provide a basis for an identity that the practitioners are unwilling to relinquish. Here too Mrs. Hurst may have been disadvantaged: much of her identity was based on her occupational competence, her ability to help others through her work, and the recognition she received for her achievements. She found no substitute for these in retirement.

There are differences among occupations in the extent to which those who pursue them can decide the level of their involvement with work and, in consequence, whether their retirement will be gradual or abrupt. The self-employed can retire gradually by sending new clients elsewhere and by reducing their availability to old clients. In contrast, for many executives the boundary between work and retirement is sharply defined: on Friday they are employed; on the next Monday they are retired. Mrs. Hurst's retirement was of this sort: she simply stopped being her agency's head.

Retirement may mean something different for men and women as a result of differences in the meaning to them of participation in the community of work. Some evidence indicates that men do somewhat better immediately after leaving work, perhaps because they less often found work to be supportive, but women do somewhat better in the long run, perhaps because of their greater ease in establishing new social relationships. In general, however, differences between the retirement experiences of men and women do not seem to be great, if one holds aside the major issue of the financial problems of many single retired women.[18]

Mrs. Hurst's retirement income was entirely adequate to her needs. Actually, the most important aspect of income for most retirees is whether there is enough of it to sustain the standard of living to which they are accustomed. Income also helps determine the kinds of experiences someone can have in retirement: it takes disposable income to afford a cruise to the Bahamas and a lot of disposable income to afford an African safari.

Mrs. Hurst also was untroubled by illness. She had no difficulty in leaving her home to do whatever she wanted to do. For some retirees the deterioration of health brings about a deterioration of morale.

Despite the bases for different experiences in retirement, all retirees face the same two challenges of retirement: to manage its threat of marginality and to utilize its promise of freedom. How these twin challenges are dealt with decides the quality of life in retirement.

In this book I have tried to describe the experience of retirement and to explain why that experience is as it is. For my fellow academics, I hope the book will provide a context for what would otherwise be the scattered probings of survey studies and economic research. For my fellow retirees, and for those who are about to become fellow retirees, I hope the book will strengthen their ability to make their retirements go well. And for those who just want to understand what it means to be retired, I hope this book will do what good travel books do: make vivid what it is like to be there.

TABLE 1
Sample characteristics: Occupation

		Number	Percentage (%)
1. Professional		34	38
Physician	5		
Lawyer	8		
Academic	11		
Nurse	3		
Other	7		
(social worker, architect, minister, accountant, city planner)			
2. Editor or publicist		6	7
3. Scientist or engineer (including software designer)		5	6
4. Administrator or manager		21	23
5. Small-business owner		10	11
6. Support personnel (purchasing agent, office manager, lab technician, bookkeeper, office worker)		6	7
7. Other (organizational consultant, sales representative, real estate broker, international businessman, janitor, craftsman, events director)		7	8
Total		89	100

TABLE 2
Sample characteristics: Sex, marital status, age

		Number	Percentage (%)
1. Sex	Male:	56	63
	Female:	33	37
2. Marital status	Married:	71	80
	Not married:	18	20
3. Age range at retirement:		60 to 70	
4. Average age at retirement:		63	

Chapter One

Reasons for Retirement

Americans tend to believe that somewhere in their early to mid-sixties they will retire.[1] Retiring before age fifty-five or so would be seen by most as retiring early, and working much past sixty-five would be seen as a stubborn and somewhat odd clinging to work (Supreme Court justices excepted).

The idea that retirement can be expected as a stage in one's life is relatively new. William Graebner, in his *A History of Retirement: The Meaning and Function of an American Institution, 1885–1978,* writes that toward the close of the nineteenth century 70 percent of white males over sixty-five were gainfully employed. People expected to work until they could work no longer. The institutionalization of retirement as a life stage was sponsored by leaders of business and industry who wanted to move older and presumably less productive workers out of their jobs, and was accepted by union leaders who wanted jobs to be available for their younger members.

Today, managers in large firms who have passed their sixtieth birthday are likely to feel some pressure to name their retirement date. If they have not as yet proposed one themselves, they may be reminded, gently, in a performance review that they need to plan for their succession. But it is unlikely that they will need this: more and more of their age-mates will already have retired, and it can be uncomfortable to play a holdout older person in a firm staffed by the young.

In the professions and the academic world, it can take longer before continuing to work elicits surprise, but it will happen there too. Nor is it only within the workplace that pressure to retire occurs. At some point most of one's friends will have retired, and may report being pleased to have done so. And one's children and spouse, sooner or later, will begin suggesting that the time has come to take it easy.

That retirement is now seen as a normal stage of life does not, of course, make retirement an obligation. But the pressure to retire that comes with that view is often augmented by a potential retiree's sense of retirement as something approaching a right. Not being able to retire because of debts or a limited or nonexistent pension, together with inadequate savings or the expenses of a child still in school, can make for a sense of things having gone badly, almost of being cheated.

The couple we interviewed who could not afford retirement owned a small business and had brought in a partner in the belief that the partner would eventually buy them out. But the relationship with the partner soured and they were forced to buy the partner out. The result was heavy debt and a need to continue working. They talked with some bitterness about friends who traveled and about having had to relinquish their own retirement plans.

The expectation of an adequate pension or a belief in the adequacy of savings, although necessary if retirement is to seem feasible,[2] usually is not enough in itself to motivate retirement. To be sure, knowing that a pension will be paid on retirement can make it seem foolish to forego potential income by continuing to work. And should people discover, as sometimes happens, that their potential pension income together with Social Security would come close to matching their current pay, they may well decide that working makes no sense. But usually financial considerations have more to do with the timing of retirement than with whether people decide to retire.

Most of those whom we interviewed were aware that Social Security payments are set so that if they have an average lifespan, their lifetime income from Social Security would be maximized by retiring at sixty-five. In general, retiring earlier than sixty-five would mean more years of payments but not enough more years to compensate for smaller checks; retiring later than sixty-five would result in larger checks but not enough larger to compensate for fewer years of receipt.

Actually, a few respondents in our study calculated that retiring at sixty-four rather than sixty-five would reduce their expected aggregate income from Social Security only a little, and chose to retire at sixty-four. Other respondents decided that maximizing aggregate return from Social Security just was not that important and chose their retirement date without reference to its effect on their Social Security payments.

Pressed to explain why they decided to retire, some retirees noted that their financial calculations told them that they were able to retire and in addition they wanted to retire. Explaining why they wanted to retire, they usually offered more than just one reason.[3] Some said, for example, that they wanted more time to be home with the family, but in addition there were problems on the job.[4]

Consider, for example, the account given by Mr. Mathers, a former sales manager in a medium-sized firm. Our first interview with Mr. Mathers took place just after his retirement. When we asked how his retirement had come about, Mr. Mathers's immediate response was that he realized he could retire at sixty-four rather than sixty-five without much of a reduction in his Social Security income, and so he decided that retiring early would not be foolish.

I retired at sixty-four instead of waiting until sixty-five because the difference in Social Security between retiring at sixty-four and at sixty-five was a very, very small amount.

But why retire at all? Mr. Mathers said that he had disliked the commute to work. A little further into our interview, however, Mr. Mathers mentioned that some five years earlier he had had a coronary bypass. He had then been fifty-nine and too young to retire. But his health became a worry.

Five years ago I underwent bypass surgery. I had a triple bypass. And I had been counseled by my cardiologist and also my general practitioner that I should learn to take it easy and relax, and that would give me a better longevity.

But in the business I was in, it is one of extreme competition and extreme pressure. And I felt at times that the pressure was affecting my health. My stomach was bothering me. And there were many times when I just felt that I couldn't sleep at night.

Not being able to sleep is a stress symptom, an expression of per-sisting mobilization to deal with what is felt to be continuing threat. The threat, in Mr. Mathers's case, was that something would go wrong at work. In any event, he could hardly avoid recognizing that his work did not permit him to "take it easy and relax."

Yet Mr. Mathers wanted to keep working. He was an effective sales manager. He had been with his firm, which catered food supplies to large institutions, since its beginnings. The firm's founder and chief ex-ecutive trusted him and permitted him almost total autonomy in di-recting the sales department. His recommendations of sales strategies were respected and generally implemented.

Then, about four years after Mr. Mathers's bypass operation, the firm's chief executive decided to reduce his own workload by bringing in his son to run the firm's day-to-day operation. Although in the past Mr. Mathers had reported directly to the chief executive, he was now asked to report to the son. Mr. Mathers's relationship with the son de-veloped badly.

The boss's son came in as the general manager, a very diligent, hardworking young man who did things his way. He would do things without really con-sulting with me that affected my department and affected the management of the company, where heretofore his father would always say, "We're going to do this; what do you think about it?"

Changes were going on as far as the sales department were concerned that I was not supportive of. I could see the sales slipping because of the pa-rameters that they were instituting about credit and things like that. Changing the compensation for the salesperson—I really felt in my heart that this could have a very serious effect on the company as far as losing some top, good, key, profitable people. I had some of these salespeople talk to me—not *some* of them, *all* of them—about their apprehensions about this.

Also, I could see where the company had made a determination that they were going to stay where they are. The building that they are currently in can-not support an additional three, five, or seven million dollars' worth of sales. They should have been looking for capital. But they said we've got to retrench. So that was a determining factor, too.

For the first time in his career, Mr. Mathers felt unwanted in the firm.

It may have been a figment of my imagination, but I felt that as far as the son was concerned, he would feel a little more comfortable if I was not in the position that I was in. I sort of got the feeling that he would like to have his own people in there. And I said, well, maybe it's time. So in December I notified the president of the company that, as of March, I had intentions of retiring.

Here we have the immediate reason for the retirement. There was the commute and there were health problems, but when Mr. Mathers saw himself sidelined by the chief executive's son, it was time to get out.

Similar stories appear in many of our transcripts: someone has reached retirement age, there are reasons for retiring but also reasons for continuing to work, but then something happens that tips the balance toward retirement. The "something" that happens can be aging that makes the job more difficult or a conflict on the job or any number of other things, including a nudge from the workplace.

The range of reasons respondents offered for the decision to retire suggests the many different pathways that converge on retirement. The process of retiring can have starting points that include, to name a few, the desire to take charge of one's time, the desire to share a leisured life with an already retired spouse, and the need to escape an embattled work situation. Retirement can be seen by retirees as opportunity or haven or reluctantly accepted exile from the world of work.

A listing of what appeared to be the primary reasons for our respondents' retirement appears as table 3. (See end of chapter.) The remainder of the chapter discusses each of the reasons.

Attractions of Leisure

Wanting the freedom to do something new

About a fifth of our sample wanted to retire not so much to leave their jobs as to gain retirement's leisure. They were ready for something new. Some had plans to travel or to pursue a hobby. More had imprecise anticipations: they would fix up the house, maybe do some painting or carpentry; they would travel or visit museums and galleries; they would see more of their children and grandchildren. Some anticipated only taking it easy, but that was what they wanted to do.

Only five respondents retired with concrete plans for the use of the time that retirement would make available. One, an academic, had agreed to provide lectures at a number of universities and had also contracted to produce a small book by a certain date. Two other academics had plans that did not work out: one planned to write a text, the other to teach evening courses. The first actually involved himself in voluntary work and in care of a second home; the second was able to carry out another of his plans for retirement—leadership of student tours of European historic sites. An accountant had been taking courses that would enable him to serve as a lay minister and had already, before his retirement, made arrangements with his church for an appointment. And a small-business owner retired in order to pursue woodworking as a serious commitment. In many ways his was a model retirement. (An extensive account of the experience of this respondent, Mr. Gilbert, is presented as chapter 8.)

Wanting leisure was not inconsistent with continued investment in work. One respondent, Mr. Fletcher, a former real-estate broker, decided after a second heart attack that if he did not begin his retirement soon he might never have it at all. He had rather vague plans to travel. But after his retirement he continued to appear at his office once a week. He liked talking with the other brokers and being able to sit at his desk, where he would make calls to prospects or, more often, to friends. He did this despite overhearing the receptionist tell callers that he had retired.

Family obligations

Nine respondents, all but one of them women, retired primarily because of family obligations.[5] In most cases their husbands had previously retired and now wanted their wives' companionship.

One of the women who retired to be with a retired husband was Mrs. Aubrey, a former city planner. Two years before her retirement Mrs. Aubrey had lost her position as head of a municipal planning bureau when a new administration abolished her office. Her husband, who was already retired, wanted her to retire then, but she instead sought new work where she could demonstrate her continued competence. She did not want her last job to be one she had been pushed out of. After two successful years in the new job, her self-confidence restored, Mrs. Aubrey retired to be with her husband.

Women who retired to be with their husbands seemed often to have mixed feelings about doing so. They tended to be younger than their husbands and felt that their retirement was a bit rushed. Had it not been for their husbands, they would have worked a few more years.[6]

Ambivalence about relinquishing work to join a retired husband is evident in the account given by another woman who retired to be with her husband. Mrs. Whitney, a former obstetrical nurse, had felt guilty when at work because of the knowledge that her husband was alone and at loose ends. But for a few months after her retirement, she missed the work and consoled herself with the thought that she might still return.

I wanted to retire when I wanted to, but I could see that when my husband retired he couldn't be alone, so I retired. I wasn't quite ready, but then I felt that we were coming to those years that I should begin to relax and I had been working for a long time and it seemed okay to retire. But it was like I wasn't retiring, that I was still going back. It was just taking a vacation. It wasn't as if this was it and I wasn't going to work anymore. It took time to realize that I wasn't going to go back to work.

Two women retired to provide a relative with nursing care. In one instance it was the respondent's husband; in the other it was the respondent's mother. The respondent who retired to be with her ill husband, Mrs. Alvarez, had headed the bookkeeping office for an investment firm. She had long planned to retire at sixty-four, when her husband, who would then have reached sixty-five, would also retire. But when Mrs. Alvarez was sixty-two her husband suffered a heart attack, and the aftereffects left him too weak to work. At that point Mrs. Alvarez told her boss that she would retire in six months. Her boss, unprepared for her departure, asked her to continue part time or at least to be available to help whomever he hired to take her place. Mrs. Alvarez remembered having been passed over for promotion several times because she did not have an advanced degree and, with some satisfaction, said no, she would not reduce the time with her husband.

The one man who retired because of familial obligations was an academic administrator who wanted to be available to an ill wife. Making it easier for him to decide on retirement was his irritation with a superior who had refused to approve his nomination of a job candidate. It was unclear whether he would have retired because of his wife's condition alone.

Disabilities

Feeling too old for the job

Feeling too old for the job can mean a number of things: losing the endurance required to work into the night; losing the patience to listen attentively to a client's complaint; losing the energy to respond to work problems quickly and appropriately throughout the day. Or it can mean feeling that one's skills and understandings have gone out of date, and that one has failed to keep up with new information, new techniques, or new machines. It can also mean losing the confidence of colleagues, clients, patients, or students, as well as feeling out of touch with their concerns and watching them drift toward people who are younger. Any of these experiences may bring about self-questioning: Is it time to go?

About one in eight of our respondents decided that yes, they had become too old to continue. Among them was Mr. Crittenden, a financial institution executive. At sixty-two he felt uncomfortably old. Other executives on his level had retired. He worried that by staying in his job he was preventing younger people from realizing their potential.

I could see I was almost the oldest person at the firm. Of *course* you always had older people in the clerical jobs. We have some ladies who have been there for fifty years, and they are still working as file clerks. But in the management echelon, I could look around and see that I was getting to be the oldest person at the meeting.

And there is just an awful lot of talent pushing up from the bottom—good, sharp, people, MBAs coming out. And these people have to progress, and they can't progress if a bunch of sixty-year-olds are sitting on top of them. So, as I approached sixty-one last year and sixty-two this year, it seemed to be less of a choice that I would retire, but almost a necessity.

After his retirement Mr. Crittenden, looking back, admitted to having felt that he had lost an edge he had possessed as a younger man. In addition, he lacked the facility with computer analysis that younger people took for granted. He was of an earlier generation; he had not kept up.

I knew I wanted to retire, simply because of a situation which had been created where every meeting I went to I was the oldest person there. And I was not as effervescent or creative or gung ho as I was at forty. And some of the younger people, I recognized, had some very fine talents which I didn't have, especially in the quantitative area, where I just hadn't taken the time to keep up. So I knew that the firm did not need me.

Retirees in other fields as well reported an awareness of younger people waiting to take over. One was Mrs. Hurst, the agency head mentioned in the Introduction, who had been encouraged by her board to retire. Others were a hospital unit director and a craftsman, each regularly kidded by younger colleagues about retiring and taking it easy. A scientist retired rather than take on a project that would have required that he remain in a responsible position into his seventies. He was acutely aware that a new generation of younger scientists had already taken over direction of his field. In his retirement he attended colloquiums, just to learn about new developments, but offered no comments: his field had moved beyond him.

A sense of flagging energy sometimes makes retirement attractive. A small-business owner said that he wanted to retire because he no longer had the energy to work the long hours his business required. A humanities professor, Professor Janelle, decided to retire in her late sixties because she saw herself failing her own standards of job performance.

I'm not as physically strong as I was ten years ago, although I'm in good shape and in good health. But I used to be able to work through a whole night and write a paper and get up in the morning and maybe I have two hours' sleep—and be just as good. I need sort of seven hours' sleep now; otherwise, I tire during the day. And also my feet are getting more tired.

So physically you feel a little bit not one hundred percent able to work yourself to the limits. And I don't want to push it to the limit that the students say, well, she's no longer a good teacher, or she's slowing down.

Usually when respondents gave flagging energy as a reason for retirement, they had strong secondary reasons too. Not only had the job become harder to do; it also had lost some of its attraction. A librarian retired because she was fatigued by her work, but in addition she felt that she had been passed over for promotion and did not want to work for her new superior. A government official, while describing herself as running out of energy and no longer invested in her work, was also being pressed by her husband to join him in retirement. A technical writer and editor said he no longer had the energy for the work, but conflicts with management, although apparently resolved, had reduced his commitment to his firm.

Illness or physical disability

About one in eight of our respondents retired primarily because of illness or disability, almost all of them because of a condition that might be seen as age-related. Two had been weakened by cancer, two retired after heart disease was diagnosed, and three had heart attacks that led them to retire. (Heart attacks were not uncommon in our sample. Another six respondents returned to work after having heart attacks and a seventh had a heart attack after his retirement.) A college professor retired because of rapidly worsening Parkinson's. A minister retired because his eyesight had entirely gone. An agency head retired because of embarrassing lapses of memory; although she had not obtained medical corroboration, she feared that the memory lapses were symptoms of early Alzheimer's.

But not every illness or disability was age-related. In particular, a financial consultant was forced into retirement by injuries incurred in an auto accident. He would have had to leave work in any case; it just happened that he was old enough to retire. Mrs. Pierce, a marketing manager, was put on disability leave by her firm after a bout of transient amnesia—quite possibly brought on by stress—and remained on disability leave for two years until she chose to retire.

In a few instances the decision to retire stemmed not from a specific illness but rather from a more general sense of physical decline. Health problems became intimations of mortality. This was the case with Mr. Evans, a former engineer who suffered a series of illnesses. Before his first illness he had given no thought to retirement. He was then sixty-two. But that first illness was followed by a year of hospitalizations and surgeries, one after another, at the end of which Mr. Evans decided that if he was ever going to retire, he had better do it soon.

I had no intentions of retiring. I went in for a hip operation; I had a right hip replaced. I intended to go back to work.

In the interim, while I was recovering from the hip, I developed a swelling on the side of my neck. I had it checked out and it turned out to be lymphoma. So they operated on that and I was to start chemo. Before they were able to start chemo, they had to run all kinds of tests and they found I had three aneurisms in the stomach, in the main artery. So they had to take care of that.

So once that was over with, again we were going to start chemo, and I had trouble with the circulation in my legs. So they had to do another operation. And with that, plus the cancer, and with chemo facing me, I decided it was enough. I decided that it was time to turn in the old tool kit and call it quits. So I officially retired.

It wasn't really my physical condition. It was the idea that if I have these many things wrong with me, and being so close to the retiring age, I said "Why push it beyond this? Let me have a few years where I can relax, or whatever. Maybe there's more wrong in there. Or maybe these things won't be as successful as they think. So let me have a few years on my own, possibly."

Often when illness or disability precipitated retirement, secondary reasons supported the decision. Mr. Winsett, the former minister, was forced into retirement by blindness, but his decision to retire was strengthened by other considerations.

To explain his retirement Reverend Winsett began, of course, with the blindness, but then went on to talk of the stress of his work:

We were very active in the pastorate, preaching twice on Sundays, Thursday night Bible studies, and working six days a week visiting folks in hospitals and homes and things like this. My eyesight's just been getting worse over the years. I'm legally blind.

The deacons of the church and other people in the church would assist in the pulpit. They would do the reading, because I couldn't see to read. I had a reader; a lady from our congregation came every week to read to me. My wife did most of the driving and visiting with me. And I had come to the conclusion it was just getting too much for her—as well as too much for me. It was frustrating, not being able to do things perhaps as you would like to do them because of your handicap.

In addition, the work was stressful:

And I just felt that it would be better to not have, in a sense, the strain of—week by week, week by week—having to prepare and preach every week, if you feel like it or not.

And there were yet other reasons for retiring. Reverend Winsett believed the time had come for a younger person to take over. And he thought that age sixty-five was the right time to leave because he would then maximize his lifetime income from Social Security.

After being in one church for forty-two years, it was time for a change for the people and a time for a change for us. Being older, we just thought it would be good, if the church wanted to, to have a younger man come as pastor. What I mean by that is that it's good for them to have a change of a person or personality.

And I figured, well, sixty-five is maximum Social Security. I want that. My wife will be sixty-two; she'll get 37½ percent of what I get. We felt that it was a good point at which to retire.

Three respondents had left work because of disability but then shifted their status to retired. Two had become clinically depressed— one after the death of a spouse, the other without apparent external cause. Each chose to retire rather than to return to work. The third was Mrs. Pierce, the former marketing manager who had been on disability leave for two years. She had hoped to return to work. She decided on retirement, however, partly because she suspected that the firm did not want her back and partly because she and her husband were running through their finances and her retirement pension would be larger than her disability check.

Other investigators have noted that health problems can be a reason for remaining at work, should work provide a sustaining community, a needed income, or a generous health plan.[7] Several respondents in this study continued working for a few years despite health problems. A professor with Parkinson's worked until problems in walking meant she could no longer trust herself to get to class. Six respondents continued to work after heart attacks. (Mr. Mathers was in this group.) It would seem more accurate in their cases to say that they worked despite their health problems, not because of them, but even quite serious health problems do not necessarily speed retirement.

Wanting To End Work

Disliking an aspect of the job

About an eighth of our respondents retired to escape from their jobs. Three—a scientist, a computer engineer, and a teacher—said only that they were tired of the work. They had done the jobs long enough. A few retired not because of the work itself as much as because of the job's conditions. One was an engineer who was irritated that new management, in an effort to reduce costs, let his building go cold. Another was a bank officer who actually liked her job but was faced with a transfer to a distant branch and a very long commute. Four of the five physicians we interviewed retired because of disliking a secondary aspect of their practice: one said he was fed up with hospital regulations, two were put off by HMO forms and requirements, and the fourth, a surgeon, had begun to see every new patient as a possible lawsuit. Retiring to escape the job can be seen as a kind of quitting. It is as if the retiree had said, "I don't have to put up with this any longer; I can retire."

Mr. Paige, the computer engineer who said he was just tired of working, had never been especially invested in his work. So far as he was concerned, his job was only a way to earn a living; it was not something that he could be enthusiastic about. He had nevertheless been quite successful. His entire career had been with one company, and he was known and respected throughout the company. But at sixty-three he decided he had had enough.

I was getting sick and tired of working. I never really disliked my job overall. There were individual phases of it and there were some departments that I worked in that I didn't like, and there were bosses that I didn't get along with. Overall I didn't dislike the work. But I never felt that I couldn't wait to get in in the morning. I went because I had to.

Programming can be a nit-picking business. You've got to do everything right. You've got to cross all the t's and dot all the i's. And it gets wearing after a while. And if it doesn't work and at two o'clock in the morning it fails somewhere when they are running a payroll or something like that, you get a call, at two o'clock in the morning, "Come in here and fix the damned thing." And that gets wearing too.

I finally decided, after about twenty-six years of programming, I was just fed up with doing it. And, why not retire? My intention has always been that as soon as I got to a point where I thought I could do it financially and mentally that I would retire. So when the time came to retire, just "Hooray!" I was glad to be out of it.

Resolving conflict by retiring

Conflict develops easily in the workplace. There can be disputes over the goals toward which a work team should strive, competition between coworkers for position and respect, the need to put up with bullying superiors and incompetent subordinates, and anger toward work systems in which superior performance goes unrecognized. Retirements fostered by conflict at the workplace, like those fostered by dislike for the job, resembled midcareer resignations except without the cost of subsequent unemployment.

Among the ten respondents whose retirement appeared primarily motivated by desire to escape a conflict in their work situation, most often the conflict was with a superior. The ten respondents consisted of the manager of a small investment firm whose divorce from the owner's daughter required that he leave the firm, two department heads whose newly installed superiors restricted their autonomy, a lower level executive whose boss prevented him from applying for a promotion for which he felt qualified, an academic at odds with his colleagues largely over disciplinary issues, two academics at odds with their dean over administrative issues, the head of an agency department who could not bring herself to work for a newly installed superior whom she did not respect, a partner in a family business wracked by quarreling, and an office manager whose new boss was persistently critical of her performance. In some of these instances the retiree's sense of misuse by the superior made for dislike of the job.

One of the academics, Professor Rembow, had been the founding chairman of his department. He retired about a year after learning that his dean would not support the department's growth.

Decisions were made that I didn't think were necessarily in the best interest of the continuing strength of the department. There were some unfavorable tenure decisions. My recommendations, some whom I had recruited, did not get tenure. The message was "We're not going to tenure your people. We will review them, but we will not allow the department to build."

Those were conditions under which I felt I could not really effectively assure the quality of the program. And I felt disappointed in the value that was put on what I had done to move the department to where I thought it was. I thought that had not been appropriately assessed.

If that hadn't happened, I'd still be there, almost certainly. But it did happen. So, the fact that I was sixty-five gave me options that younger colleagues did not have. It was not a huge penalty financially or professionally to retire.

The conflict that Professor Rembow described was undoubtedly recognized by his dean. But conflict need not have been as open as was Professor Rembow's. Mrs. Edwards, the agency department head, had been angered by the results of a superior's reorganization plan, but seemed not to have made her anger known to the superior.

The director of the agency wanted to reorganize the agency. And he wanted to put together two departments, one which I was coordinator of. He put out a posting saying something about he wants someone with five years of experience to administer the whole damned two departments together. And so I said to him very carefully, look, unless we set up a process for how these two departments can work together and who is going to administer what piece of it, I can't see applying for the job.

A very sweet young man with all of three years of experience did apply. And I said I'm not going to work under those circumstances. I suppose that's a common story in terms of many people getting close to retirement or in the retirement years, those kinds of struggles. Of course I have all kinds of feelings of vengeance and all kinds of things.

As Mrs. Edwards suggests when she says, "Of course I have all kinds of feelings of vengeance," retiring to escape conflict can give rise to a persisting sense of having been the loser. The retiree can feel that he or she had been in the right but had nevertheless departed the field.

Workplace Initiative

Being bought out

Firms that want to reduce the size of their older workforce sometimes offer inducements to older employees to retire early. They promise enhanced retirement benefits or a bonus year of salary or an increased pension. The early retirement offer may be available for only a limited time and sometimes, to make the offer still harder to refuse, by a warning that if the offer is declined a layoff may follow.

Two respondents in our sample were bought out by generous early retirement packages. In one case the firm was doing well enough but had changed its focus and wanted to downsize some departments. In the other case the firm had been losing money and wanted to move senior figures from its payroll account to its pension account.

Mr. Canfield had been a department head in a firm that had shifted its focus from research and development to production. The shift made Mr. Canfield's department a bit of a relic.

I think that the workplace changed so much that I just didn't enjoy it anymore. I was there for thirty-six years, so you can't say I didn't enjoy it while I was there, but for the last five years, or something like that, the place just completely changed. Management changed, and it just didn't go the way I liked it to go.

We were part of a technology organization and we divested from it, and the research type of atmosphere went away. I'm not saying that the research atmosphere that we enjoyed was the proper way to run a business, but we'd have big softball games and things like that, picnics and big barbecues, and things like that. And it brought everybody together. Everybody knew everybody else. It was just like a great big family.

But it didn't end up that way. Instead of the camaraderie that we enjoyed when we were looser and management wasn't as strict, they came down and started being strict. Which was probably the business way to do it, but it was just, all of a sudden, a changeover from one thing to another.

If it had stayed the way it had been, I think I'd have stayed. But they made me an offer, and my wife and I talked to a financial adviser and he said take it.

Dr. Metcalf had been a research scientist in the money-losing firm. He was taken by surprise by the early retirement offer but after some deliberation accepted it. On the day he was leaving his building for the last time, he stopped to talk with other members of the firm who had also accepted the early retirement offer. Although they all believed the deal they had been given was a good one, their feelings were mixed.

There was a slight sense of rejection from the company, because quite obviously what they were trying to do was to get rid of the older, higher-priced people so that they could save money. Just about everybody who retired was over fifty, and many were much older than that. So there was a slight feeling that, okay, we've been turfed out, maybe as a money-saving proposition. And I was thinking about that a bit. I sort of got a little angry.

I wasn't unique in that. I mean I talked to some of the other guys, and they all found that to some extent. But, anyhow, the feelings are definitely assuaged by money. So if they've got to do it, they did it about as well as it could be done.

Mr. Canfield had been ready to retire anyway, but Dr. Metcalf had not. For Mr. Canfield the early retirement package was a windfall. For Dr. Metcalf it was an offer he could not refuse but wished had not been made. In each case the buyout produced a retirement in which, perhaps surprisingly, there was some bitterness. In Mr. Canfield's case the bitterness stemmed from the realization that the happiness he felt at being bought out meant that his job had changed for the worse. In Dr. Metcalf's case it stemmed from a sense of not being valued.

Being nudged out or pushed out

Despite the illegality of a firm's requiring someone to retire, assuming that he or she can still do the work, it remains possible for superiors to push an older employee into retirement. In addition to offering an early retirement package backed by the threat of job loss, they can make the employee's job situation unpleasant and, if that doesn't produce the retirement they want, they can put together grounds for the employee's dismissal. The employee's task then is to contest the dismissal and perhaps to achieve retirement, with its benefits, as a compromise.

Nine of our respondents—about ten percent of our respondents—retired in response to pressures from their firms. With four the pressure was more a nudge than a push. An academic in her late sixties was told by her dean that part-time teaching would be available if she were to retire but that he could guarantee nothing if she decided to stay on. A manager was asked in a performance review whether he had chosen his successor. A technician was told by his boss, in a friendly enough fashion, that he lacked the skills for his job and should retire. And a respondent who had been an account manager in an advertising firm was made to feel like an outsider by his much younger peers, who regularly went to lunch together, with the respondent pointedly uninvited. The firm's head was aware of the practice and did nothing to discourage it. In each case the nudging was effective.

In addition, a respondent retired as a result of a process in which the respondent and his firm progressively distanced themselves from each other. The respondent began the process by mentioning to a superior that he was thinking about retirement. The superior and other executives then began treating the respondent as if he were on his way out the door. The respondent reacted by actually retiring.

The academic, Professor Jameson, was a professor of humanities whose dean wanted her to retire so a younger person could be hired in her stead. In a discussion about another matter, the dean asked her what were her plans. She said she hoped to continue teaching, and the dean then asked if she had considered retirement. Professor Jameson could have hung on. She had tenure, and the law prohibited forced retirement. But the dean controlled what would happen when Professor Jameson eventually did retire: whether she would have an office and be offered a course to teach. There was also an issue of the benefits she would have after retirement. The dean could influence the level of the university's contribution to her health plan. Taking it all together, Professor Jameson thought she should schedule a retirement date.

The administration likes you to retire because financially they don't have to pay such high salaries. They can get a faculty member with a lower salary. I could, legally, have put a very heavy insistence on continuing to teach full time. There is a law; you don't have to retire. But I felt it wasn't wise, in order to be on good terms with my dean, with the institution.

They offered me half-time teaching plus benefits: health and other benefits. Of course, at half time I get only half salary. But I get the full benefits, both pension and health insurance, which makes it worthwhile. The health insurance is very expensive, and they pay the full health insurance.

I could have insisted on my legal rights and said I want to go on teaching, but I weighed it both ways and I think all around it's better this way.

The manager, Mr. Reynolds, had been in charge of one of his firm's divisions when he was asked, in his performance review, to describe his plans for succession. We talked with him just after the performance review. He described the different ways in which he had been made aware in the performance review and in his job situation that his retirement would be welcomed.

I've not really been feeling like I wanted to set the date of my retirement, and now I have the feeling that I'm probably having it set for me, in a sense, even though it hasn't been set. Just reading the tea leaves. When the senior VP of personnel says you've got to find something to do that makes you worth your salary, which is the way it was put to me, that tells me that if you don't find something to do that's worth the salary, that they're going to do something about it.

And there have been a number of committees that have been formed in this new section where it would have been a logical place to put somebody where they really do have experience, and that they could have placed me in. They didn't. I've gone from being involved in almost every important place in the company to being involved almost in none of them. Zero. It's kind of gone from all to nothing.

I'll be sixty-four next month. Most people think of sixty-five as the retirement age. It's not, really, legally. I probably would not think about retirement if it hadn't been for all this.

Four respondents weren't so much nudged out, as were Professor Jameson and Mr. Reynolds, as they were forced out. One was Mr. Hindes, a mid-level manager in a public utility whose boss overloaded him with assignments and, when he left some of the assignments undone, told him that his performance was unsatisfactory and that he should retire. He recognized that he was being threatened with dismissal for unacceptable job performance, and he scheduled a retirement he did not really want.

A second respondent who was pushed into retirement, Mr. Archer, had been the publicity director for a voluntary organization. The executive director of the organization told him that she wanted him to leave. Mr. Archer never knew why.

The executive director called me in and said, well, as you know, I've been unhappy with your work, blah, blah, blah, this type of thing. And I'd like to be able to come to some sort of arrangement to let you bow out of here gracefully. And she offered me a not overly generous package. I was ready to go with no package. And so I said fine. And I wound up with something like three or four months' pay in addition to their continuing putting into my retirement and paying my hospital and medical insurance for four months.

Mr. Archer, who was sixty-two, told his coworkers that he was retiring. His coworkers brought a cake to the office, had an informal retirement party during working hours, and wished him well. He looked for another job for a bit, then decided that he would indeed retire.

Finally, two respondents, one a physician employed in industry, the other the head of public information for a foundation, were fired by bosses with whom they had been feuding. Each eventually succeeded in having his status shifted from dismissed to retired. The physician achieved this as part of the settlement of a lawsuit he brought against the firm. The publicist achieved it by appealing to his foundation's board.

Mr. Goodall, the fired director of public information, had been hired by a committee of the foundation's board and thought of himself as acting for the committee rather than for his organizational superior, the foundation's executive director. Several times Mr. Goodall had opposed programs sponsored by the executive director because they were negatively viewed by a committee of the board. Since Mr. Goodall reported to the executive director, this was impolitic.

The committee said this is a bad program. But for whatever reason the executive director said that it should be approved. And I said no, it shouldn't. So I opposed it, based on the vote of the committee. I challenged him. And that didn't sit well. After that he began to bear down a bit on me. He wanted to know where I was going, what I was doing, what papers I was presenting. A number of other occasions, where we sort of locked horns or had our differences with regard to how programs should be handled, I was going by what the committee voted. He was against that. He wanted to make his own mark.

To Mr. Goodall's surprise—although not to his wife's—the executive director had Mr. Goodall fired. The executive director had needed the backing of the chairman of the board for the firing, and he somehow obtained it.

It happened on a beautiful Friday afternoon. I was sixty-two at the time. I had been with the organization nineteen years and eight months. And I was called down by the chairman of the board and the executive director, about eleven o'clock, and handed a letter, there in the director's office. It was a Dear John letter. I'm standing there and I couldn't believe it. I said, "So what does this mean?" The director says, "You're terminated. You have until five o'clock to leave the building. Turn in your keys before you leave."

It was devastating—a great setback for me, a great setback for my wife. I just felt as though I had been condemned without a fair trial. I said to the executive director and the board chairman, "Don't I have any rights? Don't I have any right to confront my accusers?" "No, you have no rights." It felt so traumatic that I just wasn't thinking. I should have just walked out, tore the letter up, and said, "I'll see you in court."

Mr. Goodall did in fact consult a lawyer. He learned, as others have, that it is difficult to win a case on grounds of age discrimination. And legal action can be costly.

I went to hire a lawyer and the lawyer said, "Well, it will cost you a fortune because they can have all kinds of fancy lawyers who can tie you up for years and years." He told me I would not win that much in the long run, and it would be difficult for me to prove that I was told that I was too old for the job, that they wanted somebody younger and newer to come in and take my job. I would never be able to prove that unless I had witnesses.

But the committee of the board came through for Mr. Goodall. They recognized that he had been fired partly because he had advocated for their positions in his disputes with the executive director, and they were able to convince the full board (despite the opposition of its chairman) that Mr. Goodall's termination should be changed to a retirement.

Members of the committee went before the board and said look, this is wrong, the man is retired, not terminated. Fortunately, enough people on the board knew what the circumstances were, and the next board meeting they overturned the ruling of the executive director. They said, "Mr. Goodall is retired and he's entitled to his full pension rights and he's given a vote of thanks for his services." I was given my severance pay and I was given my pension and I got a letter from the executive director saying that the board had ruled that I was retired.

It is only a minority among our respondents for whom retirement was an immediate result of a nudge or push. But still other respondents reported some level of pressure to retire, although they said that it wasn't the primary reason for their retirement. One executive in a financial institution was left without job assignments; he had planned to retire anyway, and the absence of assignments only served to make him uncomfortable during his last months at work. An editor of a house journal had been asked by her boss in two successive planning sessions whether she had yet reached retirement age. When she said that there no longer was a retirement age, her boss proposed that she consider going on half-time. Mrs. Hurst, as was noted earlier, although she retired primarily because she felt it was time for her to do so, had been asked to consider retirement by her agency's trustees. And in one instance pressure to retire came entirely from peers: the skilled crafts-man in our sample was repeatedly asked by his younger coworkers, in a kidding fashion, when he would retire and make it possible for one of them to have his job. Although the great majority of retirements are entirely voluntary, some are, to say the least, encouraged.

Retirement as an Alternative to Unemployment

Six respondents who were without work for other reasons called themselves retired in preference to unemployed. These included two self-employed management consultants whose clients had stopped giving them assignments, a woman who helped run a family business who decided to stop drawing a salary because the business produced too little income to justify her continued work, and a respondent whose firm, a national retail chain, closed the outlet for which she was the financial officer, leaving her stranded. Another respondent, an office manager for a physician, decided to consider herself retired when the physician for whom she worked retired and closed the office. Finally, a former lawyer, Mr. Foster, who had gone many years without legal work, decided on reaching sixty-five that he could legitimately declare himself retired. About twenty years before his retirement, his successful legal career had been interrupted by alcoholism. He had, thereafter, had some discomfort in responding to questions about his occupation. He was pleased to become one of the retired.

On Becoming Retired

In thinking about retirement we tend to imagine a fairly straightforward process. A member of the labor force anticipates eventually retiring and begins to prepare for it with more and more focus as he or she moves from being forty-something to being fifty-something. At some point it makes sense to set a retirement date, taking into account pension rules, Social Security rules, health status, and plans for the use of retirement time. A visit to the personnel office follows and then, at an appropriate time, retirement occurs. Some people, perhaps most, do follow this scenario more or less. But many do not. They retire because they are needed at home, whatever may have been their plans, or because they have become ill, or because they are newly fed up with the job. Or they may be bought out or nudged out or pushed out.

There are many ways of entering retirement. Perhaps as with any life transition, we may imagine a single path leading to it, but the reality is much more diverse and complex.

TABLE 3
Leading reason for retirement

	Number	Percentage (%)
A. ATTRACTIONS OF LEISURE		
1. Wanting the freedom to do something new	18	20
2. Family obligations or desire for more time with family	9	10
B. DISABILITIES		
3. Feeling too old for the work	12	13
4. Illness or physical disability	12	13
C. DESIRE TO LEAVE WORK		
5. Disliking an aspect of the job or feeling burned-out, bored or stressed	11	12
6. Conflict on the job that could be resolved by retirement	10	11
D. WORKPLACE INITIATIVE		
7. Being bought out	2	2
8. Being nudged out or pushed out	9	11
E. RETIREMENT AN ALTERNATIVE TO UNEMPLOYMENT		
9. Employment ended or reduced and retirement an alternative to unemployment; retirement replaced long-term unemployment	6	7
Total	89	100

Chapter Two

The Departure from Work

Depending on their jobs, workers make the transition to retirement in a way that may be either clear-cut—on Friday they were employed; on Monday they were retired—or blurred, with no single moment at which the transition can be said to have happened. Most who are salaried have clear-cut retirements, but for those who are self-employed the boundary between work and retirement can be blurred and movement into retirement gradual.

Mr. Vella, a self-employed contractor, approached retirement by first giving responsibility for the firm's construction projects to his sons while retaining responsibility for management of the firm's real-estate holdings, then later passing on responsibility for the real-estate holdings but retaining as his personal concern the firm's small snowplow business. Then finally he became fully retired by giving the snowplow business to a grandson and leaving for the South. While in the South he briefly considered buying another business. Other retirees who had been self-employed found still other approaches to gradual retirement, perhaps reducing their work hours or taking a leave to test retirement before actually retiring.[1]

Some whose retirements were clear-cut nevertheless only gradually accepted that they were retired. Mrs. Whitney, the former nurse who left her work to be with her retired husband, at first believed that she would return to work. Only as she became more settled into her life at home did it become evident to her that she had genuinely retired.

Mr. Fletcher, the former real-estate broker, continued to appear at his office once a week despite having little to do there.[2]

Nor need retirement be once and for all. Retirees who have accepted that they are retired can unretire. A manager of a medical office had been retired for a few weeks when her former coworkers called to say they were swamped and to ask if she would return to help out. She did, and then, after a few weeks, retired again. Mr. Vella, the former contractor, became uneasy when his sons seemed to be swamped by an important project. He returned home to take charge of the project and was its full-time director until he had established that it was going well.

Both clear-cut and blurred retirements—and retirements that are then undone—can come about as a result of processes that can be orderly or, alternatively, abrupt or conflictual. An orderly process is one that moves in a predictable fashion from early planning to actual retirement. Its course is understood and accepted by the retiree and the retiree's coworkers.[3] The retiree has a sense of control over events. Each step along the way makes sense. Orderly retirements enable retirees to inform colleagues, honor work obligations, and move out of their firms with grace and a sense of continued mutual loyalty. Orderly retirements turn out to be easier for retirees to live with once they have left the workplace for good; they establish that the years of commitment to the firm and the work group were justified.

An orderly retirement might begin early in the career of the eventual retiree with adoption of a financial plan that will make retirement affordable. At first retirement may seem so far in the future that there is little real belief that it will happen, but as time goes on there is apt to be increasing awareness that it really will happen and should be planned for.[4] At some point in the prospective retiree's fifties or early sixties the prospective retiree, perhaps accompanied by his or her spouse, may talk to someone in personnel or consult a financial adviser about possible retirement incomes and when a retirement date can be set. The date would be far enough in the future for the retiree and spouse to get used to the idea and also to give superiors and coworkers time to plan for the retiree's absence.

Orderly retirements permit prospective retirees to think about what they will do in retirement. They can say good-bye to colleagues deliberately, without haste. Also, announcing a planned retirement gives coworkers a chance to prepare for the retiree's departure—though one of the ways they may do so is by treating the retiree as of diminished relevance. The coworkers will have enough time to organize retirement ceremonies: a party or lunch or combination of these that will provide some sense of caring closure to their long association with the retiree.

About half of our respondents reported orderly retirements. Among them was Mr. Ulrich, who had worked for a financial institution for thirty-eight years, the most recent ten as a project director. He had always known that he would eventually retire but he began thinking seriously about it only as he rounded into his sixties. As his sixty-fourth birthday approached, he decided that the time had come. The younger people in his group were more energetic than he and more willing to work overtime. They had computer skills he lacked, although his had been good enough until the last few years. The younger people seemed to be valued more highly by the firm's executives than he was. He was sure he could stay on in the firm if he wanted to, but he suspected that the executive group might prefer that he not.

I could have kept working, but I didn't really consider that an option. And they were getting rid of the older people, so I probably would have had my problems.

Mr. Ulrich consulted with his wife and she agreed that age sixty-five would be a good time to retire. The couple's decision regarding retirement may have been a bit easier because Mrs. Ulrich was not employed; the couple did not have to coordinate two retirements. If Mrs. Ulrich had been employed, Mr. Ulrich's retirement might have put pressure on his wife to retire, or his wife's continuing to work might have slowed Mr. Ulrich's retirement.

At this point Mr. Ulrich checked with the personnel office. What income and benefits could he expect? What else should he think about?

A year before I retired I went to Personnel and I asked them for the numbers. What am I going to get for a pension? I discussed all the decisions you have to make as far as retiring. One of the big things is, they have options which you're required to decide in terms of: what if you died the day after you retire, do you want to provide for your wife? That's a big decision. Health insurance has to be decided. I'd get Medicare, but I have to go after supplements of sorts and you have to look into that.

Mr. Ulrich said that he had concerns about different health plan alternatives and pension benefit schedules. For example, he wondered whether he should opt for a payout schedule that adjusted the payment for inflation. He wanted the Personnel Office representative to advise him on the choices he should make. He was told that although his choices could be explained to him, he had to make up his own mind. He regretted not having more guidance, but he felt that whatever he did, his pension would be enough for his needs, at least within the foreseeable future.

Mr. Ulrich then informed those with whom he worked that he planned to retire in a year.

My department, I did them the courtesy of letting them know, because I felt that was only fair. You just don't spring it on them two months before you go.

Mr. Ulrich remained a valued resource for his superiors and his colleagues. He had helped develop the firm's data management systems and was still consulted about them. But now everyone knew he was on his way out. He was not quite a lame duck, but he would not be there for the long term and asking him to take on long-term responsibilities made no sense. Although no one especially wanted it to happen, Mr. Ulrich became a more marginal member of his work team. His department head asked younger people to assume responsibilities that might once have been his.

You're telling the department head, "Hey, look. Don't give me any project that lasts more than a year, because I won't be here." That's pretty frightening to a department head. So if we were on a project, I would never be put in charge of anything, because I wouldn't be there. That contributes to the lowering of credibility and so forth. I could feel myself getting further and further away from being involved, because the people I worked with knew I wasn't going to be there.

When the time came for pay increases to be awarded, Mr. Ulrich did not receive one.

My boss had to build up other people in the department to replace me—for example, raises. Now, I was fairly high-paid, although I wasn't that high. But here's someone who is going to retire in a year, where a raise wouldn't matter. You'd get a few dollars extra during that year. Do you give that to the person that you're trying to bring up? What do you do?

The attitude of management was pretty clear. You don't put money on someone who is going to leave in a year. And I agreed. I certainly was sympathetic.

Mr. Ulrich could see things from the perspective of the work team: he understood that he would now be less central to the team's functioning. The understanding helped, but not entirely. Despite telling himself not to take the matter personally, Mr. Ulrich was distressed by what felt like diminished worth in the workplace.

A year later, having retired, and looking back on the experience, Mr. Ulrich said:

Emotion enters into it, because you know that you're no longer important. And that's something I think any older person faces, or most older people face, that you're no longer in the mainstream and therefore you've got to adjust. And some people find it very difficult, if they've had any power at all, to get in that position.

When I didn't get a raise the last year, and was not put in charge of any projects that extended over a year, I agreed with both of these. And so I had no problem—except emotionally, that you're on the skids and that the end is approaching. And that is a trauma.

My expertise, which is extensive in this particular area, would demand that I was in charge of part of a project. But you can't give him a lasting, long-term project because he's not going to be here. They couldn't give me a specific job because I wasn't going to be there.

In deference to my knowledge, they would usually listen to me. Everybody treated me with deference, as if I were important. And I wasn't. I was not a figurehead, but I had no real responsibilities. I was really acting as a consultant, although I was full time on the payroll.

It is not only the retiree's coworkers who begin preparing for the retiree's departure from the work community. Retirees also prepare themselves for their departure by cleaning out their files and by removing personal items from their offices. Retirees spoke of reversing the process of making their offices congenial environments. Instead of bringing pictures or books or plants to their offices, they began taking home those that were there. One respondent, Mrs. Caldwell, a former bank manager, described what it was like to return an office to its earlier anonymity.

I had a lot of personal things that I was taking out gradually. And as people would come into my office, they would say, "This has changed so." Somebody said, "This isn't you anymore." That was a strange feeling—all of a sudden an office without me.

In the months before his retirement Mr. Ulrich began thinking about what it would be like to have no office to go to. He worried about what he would do with himself. After his retirement Mr. Ulrich described the mixed feelings he had had.

During the year I was very apprehensive, frankly, about being through. I didn't know how I was going to react. There were times when I didn't want to be through. I don't think that you formulate any thoughts, but it's a totally different feeling than you've ever had before. Is there life after sixty-five? What the hell am I going to do with my time? You don't formulate these thoughts, but they're going through your mind.

It's always in the background. It's not exactly a cloud, but it's a mixture of joy in the fact that you're not going to have to commute, and then a little sadness because you're not going to be associating with all these people.

As Mr. Ulrich's departure date became imminent, the people with whom he worked arranged a series of what could be considered retirement ceremonies to let him know their respect for him and to wish him well in his new life. Mr. Ulrich said:

As I got closer and closer to my retirement date I went through the dinners. They took me either out to lunch or to dinner. We had dinner at a first-class hotel. There was just one small group of people, a dozen, all people mostly that I had been working with for years, and so everybody knew each other. And there was no speech making or anything like that, just a get-together. It was the kind of an affair that I like. There were several lunches in different places, various groups.

Mr. Ulrich's firm had as a practice provided a morning party for those about to retire. Even a somewhat ritualistic good-bye–saying ceremony can awaken much emotion. The ceremony makes manifest the ending of working life, of associations, of place.

Traditionally they have a morning get-together where all the people who want to say good-bye come, and you go through the routine of food and the tribute, and they usually give a gift of some kind. And you stand there for an hour or so saying good-bye. It's very traumatic. Two reasons: you don't want to say good-bye, really, and all these people displaying that much interest is a little unnerving, frankly, in my opinion.

Mr. Ulrich treated his last week at work as a transition to retirement. He hardly worked at all. What he mostly remembered doing was saying good-bye again and again.

The last week or so I didn't work very much, frankly. I came in late and left early. What was the point? I would just really disturb things if I was there. So in that time period—probably a week, I don't remember—you would be spending your time really saying good-bye, and then go on home. The last day you spend repeating your good-byes and circulating with people you know. And whether it was traumatic, I don't remember, but you had that feeling all along that you're losing something.

Retirees whose retirements were orderly tended to move into retirement easily. There were exceptions, especially among people who had relied on their community of work to fend off social isolation. But more typical was Mr. Paige, a computer engineer, who had planned his retirement for a few years. He informed his boss about a year before his chosen retirement date and at the same time informed the people he worked with. His boss was able to decide on a replacement without feeling rushed. A week before Mr. Paige's retirement date, his colleagues organized a lunch that was low-keyed and pleasant. By the close of his last day at work Mr. Paige felt entirely ready to move into retirement. When he was asked in an interview four months after his retirement, "How long did it take before you felt comfortable in retirement?" Mr. Paige replied, "As long as it took me to get to the car in the parking lot."

Our respondents varied greatly as to how diligently they worked as they approached the day of their retirement. Mr. Paige, like Mr. Ulrich, did little work in his last days in the office. Two weeks before his retirement Mr. Paige was told by his boss not to take on anything new and to come in only as he wanted to. On the other hand, some retirees—women, especially—chose to work until the last hour of their jobs in order not to leave anything unfinished.

Men in administrative or executive positions seemed to treat their last days in the office somewhat differently than women in similar roles did. Men, more than women, seemed to act as if retirement meant that they were relinquishing their position on a team; once they had done so, they had no further responsibility to the team. Women, more than men, seemed to act as if they felt responsible for leaving their offices in good order. Like most gender comparisons, this one does not describe all men and all women, but there seemed to be tendencies along these lines.

A few retirees, all women, returned to the workplace after they were formally retired just to make sure that a project had been completed properly or that their files were in order or that they had left adequate directions for the next occupant of the office. One of them was Ms. Putnam, a college administrator, who returned to her office on weekends despite having formally retired. Her explanation to her boss was that she "had not cleaned up things the way I wanted to."

My last day I saw the director, and a couple of people who were in the director's office. He always is very gracious. And he was very gracious. And I told him that I would be around because of the fact that I had not cleaned up things the way I wanted to, and I was holding on to my keys. I would not be in Monday through Friday; I would only come in on Saturdays, because I did not want to interfere in whatever decisions were made.

Another woman among our respondents, Professor Merrill, had been forced into retirement by illness. She had put off retirement as long as she could, but finally it became too difficult for her to walk from the cab that deposited her at curbside to her office or a class. Nevertheless, she went to her office the weekend before her successor was to take it over, to make sure that the successor could easily find the information needed for the current year's program. Another respondent, Mrs. Perry, at the very end of her service as office manager in a medical practice, came in evenings to help her coworkers deal with a new filing system. None of the men in our sample reported anything like this. The closest was the continued commitment by newly retired medical and legal professionals to their patients and clients.

Ceremonies of Retirement

The term "ceremonies of retirement" might be used to refer to the retirement parties, meals, and informal conversations that are intended to deal with the emotions of ending work relationships. Ceremonies of retirement tell retirees that their contributions to their firms have been recognized and that the people with whom they have worked are steadfast in their affection and respect despite the coming separation.

Formal retirement parties have predictable elements. Dan Jacobson summarized in the following way fourteen parties for retiring employees in four Israeli organizations. Observations of retirement parties in the United States would produce similar results.

Expressions of sadness, by all the speakers and the guest of honor, at the imminent separation; ... a solemn promise to keep in touch; ... presentation of a gift; ... toasting the retiree; ... reminiscing about incidents in the retiree's life in the organization, either in the form of flattering anecdotes or praise for his or her work and devotion; ... the retiree's own reminiscences, in a semiformal farewell speech or in the form of interjections ... during the speeches made by others; ... reference ... by the retiree as to his or her future plans; ... exchanging and updating of telephone numbers and addresses with some of the participants at the end of the party, and all or some of them posing for group photographs.[5]

The ceremony might end with handshaking or hugs. The message to the retiree is that the retiree had mattered, his or her departure is accepted, and not only are there are no hard feelings, but there is continued affection.

Some respondents reported that they had resisted the idea of a retirement party. They remembered their own reluctant attendance at parties for people they had not known well. They remembered, too, questioning the sincerity of senior figures as they praised the retirees' contributions. With their own reactions to the retirement parties of others in mind, they were reluctant to be the focus of a retirement party themselves.[6] Dr. Cooper, a physicist who divided his time between teaching and research, said, before his retirement:

I know people will plan a party and all that sort of thing, and I just don't want anything like that. I've attended retirement parties and it's embarrassing, all the lies that get told, all the conflicts that get washed over and whitewashed. And I just didn't want that.

Yet the retirees in our sample who had retirement parties almost always were pleased by them, though often with some reservations. For example, Dr. Brevis, a psychiatrist who formerly directed an inpatient service, had good memories of a party given him despite his initially having said that he did not want it.

I had told my associate director months and months ago; I said, "I don't want any kind of a party when I leave." We'd had one lunch or dinner or something for one person after another who was leaving, either having lost the job or being transferred somewhere. I didn't want people to spend money on a gift and meal and so on. I really didn't. But they insisted on it anyway.

They had a retirement party for me six weeks or so after I had retired. The associate director did it. I'd been medical director of three different units, so there were people from other units invited to the retirement party. It was enjoyable, seeing all the people again, some people that I had not worked with in recent years, but several years before.

Dr. Cooper, the physicist who had initially opposed a party, was ultimately happy to be given one. Dr. Cooper had had disputes, mostly theoretical disagreements, with colleagues both in his university department and in his research group. He was pleased that those who spoke at his retirement party acknowledged the disputes yet expressed continued respect.

Once the decision had been made, okay, I'm going to retire, I told the department. I was still teaching and all that. And one day it turned out that there was going to be a party. And it was a good party. I enjoyed it.

A couple of things stand out. Looking back on twenty-five years of activity, the thing that colors the whole thing is my dissidence. And one thing that was very good was that that wasn't glossed over. I was afraid people would say, "Well, fundamentally, we all agree" and, when I've disagreed, "He doesn't really mean it." Or something like that. That didn't happen.

Somebody who used to be there, someone I respect very much, gave one of the little talks. We'd become good friends and then he left. He said that I was a national treasure. And that pleased me. I don't think I overinterpreted it. But I do interpret it as more than just a nice thing to say.

It mattered very much to Dr. Cooper that the people who spoke well of him at his retirement party were people whose respect he valued. Their talks reassured him that his contributions had been recognized.

My boss on a project I'd worked on, for whom I have a lot of respect and always have had, and we've kept in touch more or less, he came all the way from Washington. And that was nice. And he said that most of the good ideas on the project were mine, and if he made any mistakes they were probably because he ignored my advice.

And I think that the party told me that people thought well of me. And it was pretty clear to me that it wasn't just bullshit. I'd been to other retirement parties where people just groan because it's just so much bullshit. But that didn't happen.

It also mattered to Dr. Cooper that his wife and children were at the party. The demonstration for his family that his colleagues thought well of him might be seen as strengthening his claim to his family's respect. It also could constitute a kind of explanation for the time Dr. Cooper gave to his work rather than the family. Mr. Mathers, the retired sales manager, whose family also had attended his retirement party, addressed this issue.

They had a time for me at a hotel, and all of my family members were invited. They had a big dinner and presented me with some plaques and accolades. And my children were there to see this all happen.

I think it's extremely important if a man or a woman were retiring that their children be there to see their accomplishments—and not only their accomplishments but the feeling of their colleagues toward them, the respect, the understanding that fellow workers have toward them. This is not always noticed and received by the children. They say, oh, my daddy goes to work and he's a bus driver or he's a plumber or he's a carpenter; they don't know the camaraderie that is built up—and the respect.

Even spouses—sometimes spouses don't realize what a husband may do in the workplace. And as long as it can be recognized and the family members see this recognition, it means a lot. I mean, you can come home with plaques and say, "Look at the nice plaque I got" or something like that. But being there to see the feeling of the people that I worked with, this meant a lot to them.

Mr. Ulrich's experience, described earlier in this chapter, of being stirred by the morning gathering to mark his retirement, was paralleled by the experience of others. Retirement parties forcefully established that the retirees had come to the end of their careers. Nor could the retiree escape recognizing that the party was a way to say good-bye. Mrs. Caldwell said about her retirement party:

I don't know why it hit me, because I was having a good time. It just seemed like I was seeing all these people that I haven't seen for a long time that had left or had taken early retirement and they chose to come and say good-bye. I was a little weepy—weepy—just saying good-bye to all the years that I had worked with all these people, and knowing, well, I'll never see them again. Which I probably won't.

When a conflict with a senior figure had led to the retirement or at least had made retiring more attractive, the conflict was entirely hidden from view during the retirement party. Indeed, the talk honoring the retiree's service might be given by the senior figure with whom there had been conflict. Professor Rembow was among respondents who had this experience. He had retired largely because his dean refused to support his program. He was bemused when the dean turned out to be the main speaker at his retirement party.

They had the usual party by the department. It was nice. The outstanding feature really was that not only my departmental colleagues were there, but people from almost every department in the university with whom I had come in contact through committee work. The accolades were appropriate. My successor chairman was there and made some remarks. The dean was there and made his speech. I didn't value his contribution. Our disagreements, our pronounced disagreements, were part of the retirement process.

And yet, for a supervisor who had engineered or at least encouraged a retirement to be a key figure in the retirement party might not be hypocrisy. In at least a couple of instances it seemed as though once the conflict over the respondent's retirement had been resolved, the supervisor became genuinely concerned about the respondent's future. For the retiree, such a shift from conflict to concern might be inexplicable. Mr. Baker, who had been forced into retirement from his position as a public relations director, said, "The strangest thing was that after we had reached an agreement on my leaving and all this, then all of a sudden it's like the person was almost like a schizophrenic personality—that all of a sudden she's my friend and wants to talk about what am I going to do in my retirement." And Mr. Trexler, whose boss had considered him unsuited for his laboratory technician job and had urged him to retire, was surprised to discover that it was the boss who organized his retirement party. As the party's main speaker, she warmly praised Mr. Trexler.

A few retirees who said they did not want a retirement party were taken at their word. But the result, in at least one instance, was disappointment. Mr. Derwitt, a manager, had been nudged into retirement in a performance review conducted when he was sixty-three. In that review he had been asked, rather pointedly, to describe his plans for succession. Who would take over on his retirement? Did he have a date for that retirement? Although he had not thought seriously about the matter, Mr. Derwitt answered that he thought he might retire in a year or so. That tentatively offered date became a commitment: senior management began acting on the assumption that he would retire a year after the date of the performance review.

Mr. Derwitt told coworkers that he did not want a retirement party because retirement parties were empty rituals. Actually, he had another reason for not wanting a party: he hoped his company would ask him to serve as a part-time consultant after his retirement and thought that a party would make it too evident that he was no longer connected to the firm. (Two years later, when we last talked with Mr. Derwitt, no consultancy had eventuated.) Mr. Derwitt's coworkers, perhaps in response to his having said that he did not want a retirement party, did not arrange one. Nor did they take him to lunch or dinner or present him with a gift. A few colleagues came to his office to say good-bye, but that was it.

Mr. Derwitt felt hurt that despite his many years with the firm his departure was so little noted.

I was with the company thirty-seven years. And I'm sure that I'm the only person – and I was a senior officer of the company – I'm sure that I'm the only one in the company's history that left at retirement age that wasn't offered some kind of a retirement party.

I didn't want a party, actually. I've been to enough company parties; I don't need another one. I'd rather have a small group of people than one of those tremendously large affairs. But I thought it would have been nice to have an offer. I was, frankly, surprised. I think nobody thought of it. What I had intended, if it had been offered, was to take the funds and put them in something useful like the public library or something like that.

But after thirty-seven years, thinking that I had contributed a lot to the company, I got the feeling that there really was a kind of a void in the end that should have been filled in.

The ceremonies associated with saying good-bye can be occasions for much else as well. As Jacobson notes in his review of the many possible functions of retirement ceremonies, retirement parties provide coworkers with an opportunity to strengthen relationships with each other and provide management with an opportunity to announce organizational developments.[7] But for respondents whose service is honored at retirement parties, what is most important is that the party demonstrates that they mattered.

Retirements that were abrupt or unexpected

Retirements that are not orderly can happen in all sorts of ways. A sudden illness can make retirement an unexpected necessity. Or the retiree may choose to leave after failing to receive an expected promotion. Or the firm may prompt the retirement, by making an early retirement offer, perhaps accompanied by a warning that the alternative could be a layoff. Or the retiree may be forced to leave by a determined management.

Dr. Metcalf, the scientist who was bought out by his firm, had been required to retire within a month of the offer. People who retire under such circumstances, like people whose retirements result from conflict, tend not to have retirement parties; they just leave. In Dr. Metcalf's case a kind of retirement ceremony did occur. He and other senior people who had also accepted the early retirement offer found themselves standing together inside the firm's outer door on the last day of their service.

This last day was sort of weird. A lot of other senior people went. So there was this group standing in the hallway on the way out of the door, six of us. And we all sort of looked at one another and said, "Do you really believe this is happening?" It was a mass exodus of senior people.

A year after having been bought out, Dr. Metcalf viewed the organization's actions with a sense of irony. Although the early retirement offer had been generous, his appraisal of it was, "My, but they were anxious to get rid of us." He remained rankled by the firm's belief that it would be better off without him.

In truly abrupt retirements there is no possibility of a ceremony of departure. Mrs. Pierce, the marketing manager who suffered transient amnesia, experienced the amnesia on a Friday afternoon while on her way to her mother's nursing home. She worried about the amnesia over the weekend and on Monday morning presented herself to her firm's medical office. The nurse who talked with her insisted that she immediately obtain medical attention, in order to rule out stroke. Tests showed no sign of stroke. Nevertheless, Mrs. Pierce was put on disability leave. She had talked with her boss the day she was told to obtain medical attention, but was never again in her office. There were no lunches, no ceremonies to recognize her departure.

When we talked with Mrs. Pierce, about two and a half years after she left her job and six months after her formal retirement, she seemed still shocked by the suddenness of her departure from work. She had planned on an orderly retirement, not the sudden break from work she experienced. Her one source of reassurance that her years of work had not been pointless was her retirement pension.

There is a lot of difference between dropping out of the workforce without being ready for it and being retired. Being retired formally is a gentler approach than being severed from work just like that, just like an axe falling and you are severed, just like going along and getting decapitated. Retired is knowing where you are at and knowing that this is going to take place, and this is part of the life process.

I know that I've reached that age—hey, sixty is here. And I now have a few dollars coming in because I've retired. It makes it easier that all my work and all my contribution has not gone to waste. I've worked hard to be able to retire with some money.

Retirements that resembled quitting in that the retirees left their jobs in exasperation or anger—"I don't have to put up with this; I can retire"—were unlikely to be marked by anything more than a few informal good-byes. Mr. Mitchell retired after being reassigned from a supervisory position to warehouse inventory control. He viewed the reassignment as the demotion it appeared to be, and retired rather than accept it. He said good-bye to a few coworkers, and that was it. Two years later he felt he had been mistreated by the firm and also felt unhappy about having left with no one seeming to care.

An even more acrimonious retirement was reported by Mr. Williams, formerly a partner in a family business run by his older brother. The retirement stemmed from a conflict between Mr. Williams and the brother over the extent to which Mr. Williams could function autonomously. Mr. Williams said that if he could not run his department the way it should be run, he would retire. His brother said that would be fine.

Before leaving the firm Mr. Williams wanted to say good-bye to the employees who reported to him. But because he did not want to make the employees seem to be demonstrating loyalty to him rather than to the firm, he invited them to dinner at his house.

It had been agreed as to how my retirement would be done within the company. And none of the agreements were honored. Instead of my being allowed to make an announcement to my staff–I had maybe thirty, thirty-five people reporting to me–instead of my telling them, they began to tell me that "We heard you're leaving." It was leaking out. They even told me who my replacement was going to be. They knew everything.

Rather than have it happen that way, we had a dinner at my house for the people with any longevity or real responsibility, at which I announced it. There was a lot of sadness.

No respondent who had been pushed into retirement had a retirement party within the firm. A coworker who organized such a party would have seemed to be questioning management's actions. No matter how loyal fellow workers might have felt toward the person pushed into retirement, they had their own jobs to worry about. Mr. Williams understood that.

I had a green rug in my office; my brother had a brown rug. There was a green team and a brown team. If you wanted to keep your job, you were on the brown team. A lot of people were straddling the line, and it was very uncomfortable for them. There were a couple of straddlers who cried crocodile tears. But for the most part people were very sweet and very caring. They went on with their jobs–and I certainly understand that–but they genuinely cared.

Several other respondents were also pushed into retirement. Two, Mr. Goodall and Dr. Anderson, were initially fired but then were able to have the firing converted to retirement. But first both were subjected to what might be called a degradation ceremony.

Dr. Anderson had been in charge of the medical office of a large firm. His dismissal followed a disagreement with a superior over responsibility for a failure to provide immediate attention to a worker in a distant building. The superior, with whom Dr. Anderson had had previous confrontations, told Dr. Anderson his service in the medical office was over. He said that rather than return to the office Dr. Anderson should report to an outplacement service the firm had retained.

For a couple of days Dr. Anderson, almost in shock, did as he was told. When the outplacement staff said they wanted to review any call he might make to the medical office he had directed, Dr. Anderson hired an attorney. The attorney threatened to sue Dr. Anderson's firm on grounds of false allegations of misconduct leading to wrongful dismissal. The firm's attorneys, rather than have the case go to court, agreed to a settlement with Dr. Anderson. He was permitted to resign with full pension rights and, in addition, received health and dental benefits beyond those contained in the pension plan.

Mr. Goodall, who had been in charge of public relations and publications for a foundation, felt degraded in a similar way.

I didn't feel like having any lunch. I sat in my office and I looked at my papers and I began gathering up the materials that I knew I was entitled to and I just started bagging them up. And I was looking for somebody to talk to. When I went to see certain people in the organization, I saw the doors closed. They knew it was happening. They didn't want to get involved.

So I put twenty years of papers and materials that I knew that I was entitled to in the back of my car, and only the janitor—only the janitor out of fifteen people—had the courtesy and the empathy to come down and say, "I'll give you a hand." He helped me carry out the materials. When I got outside, he said, "I'm very sorry about this." He said, "I don't know what it's all about, but it's wrong."

When we talked with Mr. Goodall a year after his retirement, he remained bitter toward the organization as well as its executive director. His files were in his attic, unopened. When he thought of going through them, his anger returned. He, like Dr. Anderson, regretted having given so much of his life to a firm that had so betrayed him.

Chapter Three

Gains and Losses

An extensive literature exists on retirement's effect on well-being. What seems to emerge from that literature is a picture of an initially positive response to retirement by most retirees, followed by declining satisfaction.[1] It would seem that as retirement progresses, the retired become more vulnerable to illnesses, financial worries, bereavements and other losses, and have a sense of lessened control over their lives. But not all retirees experience this decline in well-being. Those who maintain a positive outlook seem likely to hold their own. At the least, their satisfaction with retirement persists. When worrying won't solve a problem, it helps not to worry.[2]

Orderly retirements are much more likely to go well than abrupt and unplanned retirements, at least at first. Yet an orderly retirement does not guarantee that things will thereafter go well: social isolation can be a threat, and all but the best-financed retirements are vulnerable to income shortfalls should serious illness occur. But most retirees who have had the time to prepare for retirement find it on balance a good experience.[3]

Nevertheless, even in the best of circumstances, with a sought retirement achieved after an orderly process, retirement brings losses as well as benefits. Work is rarely entirely a bad thing or entirely a good thing, and while ending work brings benefits, it brings costs as well. Some of the benefits and costs of retirement are mirror images of each other: to have the one is to have the other. For example, not being obliged to go to work makes it possible to sleep late in the morning, but the absence of work can make the day that follows seem empty. Not being responsible for demanding tasks means freedom from stress but also means not having opportunity for achievement. Although not every retiree will experience each cost and benefit to the same degree, most will have some familiarity with them all.

Costs of Retirement

It may not be until their retirement that people recognize how very much their jobs had given definition to their time and so given structure to their lives. But it was the job that decided which days they could keep for themselves and, in the other days, which hours. Without a job to take a vacation from, retirees may find that vacations lose their meaning: an extended trip that breaks routine is a time away, an adventure—but not a vacation. A work holiday like Memorial Day or Columbus Day is not much different from any other day except that it allows one to park without feeding a meter.

Before their retirement, work had segmented retirees' days—a commute, work time, a return commute, and evening at home—with abrupt shifts in settings and responsibilities between segments. In contrast, their days in retirement move seamlessly from waking to lunch to afternoon activity to dinner, evening television, and bed. Retirees stop setting their alarm clocks. They no longer need to rush through breakfast to get to the car or the bus stop. There is no special time for anything unless an appointment has been made. The job-imposed rhythm of the day simply disappears.

Having an entire day at one's disposal can impart a luxurious sense of freedom. Yet after years of organizing oneself to meet the expectations and demands of a job, now experiencing featureless days that offer nothing special to do and no place special to be can also be unsettling.[4] In an interview conducted about a year after his retirement, Mr. Ulrich, who had arranged an orderly retirement from his position as a project director for a financial institution, regretted the absence of work's structure:

The lack of structure has been my biggest problem, missing the discipline and the structure. It's amazing how easy it is to stay in bed or get into the habit of staying in bed. And this has been one of my major problems, routine.

Before I retired, I said, oh boy, I'll listen to the radio every morning and see how bad the traffic is and feel pretty smug because I don't have to cope with it. And all of a sudden there's no discipline. I just stay home. And that's upsetting.

You've been in a discipline for all of those years where Monday meant you started the week and Friday meant you ended the week and then you have two days to do everything you would normally want to do in terms of yard work and traveling or anything like that. So you more or less knew exactly what day it was. If it was somewhere between Monday and Friday, you knew how many days it was to the weekend. The big problem in retirement is remembering what day it is.

That retirees cannot remember the day of the week is a bit of an exaggeration. Even in retirement the weekends are distinct. The neighbors are home during the day, as are their children. One's own grown children may stop by, bringing the grandchildren. Television carries sports rather than weekday soaps. On Saturday the stores are more crowded, and on Sunday newspapers are thick and there's church to attend. On the other hand, the retired can maintain pretty much the same schedule on weekdays and weekends. It is just as easy to garden or to shop or to visit a fitness center on a Thursday as on a Saturday. A leisurely breakfast is just as easily managed on a Monday as on a Sunday. Although the Sunday crossword may be larger, retirees have time for the crossword right through the week.

Retirees' days are without urgency. They can get up from the breakfast table at noon if they wish. But one possible result of taking it easy is that time can escape unnoticed. At the end of the day a retiree may have done little more than run a few errands and engage in a small event: lunch with a friend or a visit to the doctor's. The rest of the day was spent at home, where he or she completed a few household chores. And yet, perplexingly, the day will have seemed full. Retirees may wonder how they ever had time for work.

The absence of obligation to be some particular place at some particular time can have a second implication: that the retiree has become marginal to the workings of the society. The obligation to be somewhere means that someone is counting on your appearance. If nobody expects you to show up, maybe it means that nobody cares, that you do not matter to anyone. This is not something retirees obsess about, but in an extended interval without obligations—a few days or a week—the thought is likely at some point to suggest itself.

The Work Itself

The psychologist Mihalyi Csikszentmihalyi coined the term "flow" for the experience of being so immersed in a task that a loss of self-awareness occurs. Having tasks in which there is flow makes days go by quickly. Most jobs—all jobs that are satisfying—provide such tasks.[5]

Occasionally retirees think back to work they had loved. For example, Mr. Mitchell, the former warehouse manager whose demotion had led him to retire, sometimes thought back to a time when he had been given a job he loved.

I was given the responsibility of finding out what pieces of equipment we needed to produce over the upcoming year, over the next two years. I had to be in touch with the group that was doing the forecasting of the major items within the corporation that they were going to sell. Once I had that, I had to go to the people who were handling our engineering parts listing system in order to relate what materials were going to be used in these various pieces. And I was bucking what was called an engineering parts listing system, which was in the throes of being revised. I loved it very much from an esthetic standpoint, an intelligence standpoint.

Dealing well with a challenging job provided Mr. Mitchell with a sense of effectiveness. Watching himself do well enhanced his self-esteem. And it was work in which he could become absorbed—in which he could experience flow.

Some respondents found pleasure in responding well to highly stressful tasks. They had enjoyed the challenge of organizing their thoughts during a difficult meeting or managing their emotions so they could deal well with a client's complaint. Mr. Taylor, a former trial lawyer, remembered with pleasure the pressures of a law practice.

Law is a pressure game all the time, all day long. When people call you or come in, it's some kind of a problem, troubles. And I thrived on it as a younger man. Cripes, I loved pressure. I really loved it. Loved it.

Sometimes I'd have two or three courts to go to in the morning, three and four cases. Didn't bother me that there was pressure in each one of them or people were waiting. It was one at a time and go. It didn't bother me. It was great.

Even though I'd been trying cases for thirty years, forty years, I never had a case that didn't worry me. Or, to put it differently, didn't cause a certain amount of tension as trial approached. And I never got into court on a trial where I wasn't really uptight until it got rolling. For all that, I enjoyed the experience. I enjoyed the trials. I had reasons to enjoy the outcomes, mostly. And on to the next one.

Mr. Taylor said he had lost some of his ability to handle pressure as he had gotten older. He had become a better lawyer in some ways—more knowledgeable, more considerate of his clients—but he was less able to bounce back from a stressful occasion. Still, he missed his practice. His retirement was without the wonderful engagement of being a lead actor in courtroom dramas. It was, in a word, dull.

Mr. Taylor was among the minority of respondents who were bored in retirement. As he put it, "I've not enjoyed the experience of the absence of tensions." Mr. Taylor had no interest in returning to work, although he still had a desk in his former law firm. Mostly he was home during the day. A few evenings during the week he attended meetings of Alcoholics Anonymous. He saw his children now and again and saw his ex-wife on rare occasions. Retirement for him was not a good time of life.

Another respondent who found retirement boring was Mr. Marquis, a former businessman. Mr. Marquis had retired from heading his own medium-sized business after his hospitalization for a heart condition. He said that retirement turned out to be almost unbearable.

I never planned on retiring. I couldn't stand the inactivity. I had nothing to do. I was quite upset. My mind was still going. I was on the phone, gabbing away, all day long. Talking to business acquaintances, friends of mine, people in business. Reading every bit of newspaper I could, magazines, trade journals, keeping abreast of what was going on in the world. And — not feeling sorry for myself — but really resenting that I was out of it.

Mr. Marquis called the president of a firm that had been his chief competitor and asked for a job, any job. He was offered a job with the firm's customer relations group. That proved entirely satisfactory.

Community

For most retirees work had sustained their sense of themselves as people with membership in a community of work, acknowledged by its other members as having a right to be among them. Retirement ended that membership and with it the relationships that it had sponsored.

No one works in isolation: the apparently lonely shoemaker has customers, suppliers, and a landlord, plus friends who stop in to pass the time of day. Work embeds people in relationships: they perform tasks assigned by superiors, respond to the requests of clients, join their efforts to those of coworkers. Just getting to the job brings about incidental contacts, opportunities for brief exchanges with people who run a newsstand or provide lunch or work in adjacent offices. All these relationships are lost with retirement. One respondent said, "It's not work that I'm leaving behind; it's the people."

Some retirees hang on to a few work relationships despite their retirement. They meet former colleagues for lunch; they may maintain a friendship with one or two. But most retirees leave their work relationships behind when they leave their firms. Many find it hard to replace the community of work. Coworkers get to know each other and, often, to develop feelings of mutual loyalty on which they learn to rely. Although they are unlikely to develop relationships of total candor— after all, they can anticipate working together a long time—they get to know each other well. Nor is it simply the work relationships, one by one, that matter; rather, it is the community in which everyone has a place, everyone is known, and throughout the community there is acceptance and respect.

For those for whom there are no relationships and communities of importance other than the community of work, to leave the community of work may seem like exile. When we last saw Mr. Taylor, about two years after he had retired, he talked about how much he missed the relationships associated with his work. It was not that he had been especially close to the colleagues and others with whom he interacted during his workday; it was that the relationships, taken together, had constituted a community he valued, within which he was a respected member.

I had a very good relationship with my fellow attorneys and with the judges. Although it was largely occupied with disagreement, dissent, adversarial activity, it was rewarding in the sense that there was a mutual respect that I felt, and I'm sure existed, a feeling of mutual respect that I had for the attorneys that I dealt with, both with and against, and the judges that I appeared before. And so it was a very pleasant and satisfying experience.

And after you have been in the same building for forty years, you get to know the people. Like there're lawyers in the building I know to say hello to, just a brief conversation. There are lawyers over the next street, by the courthouse. There are judges and clerks and others that I would see back and forth. You don't get into detailed conversation with them but at least you say hello, how are you, and what's doing, and this and that.

If you don't come into town, you don't see them anymore, and you don't say hello to them, spend the time of day with them for a minute or two.

Social life at work, as elsewhere, includes conflicts as well as alliances, and competition and disparagement as well as support. Among the benefits of retirement is escape from these. But even then, the loss of the community of work can reduce the richness of life.

Sometimes at the lunches and parties that are the good-bye ceremonies of retirement the retiree is invited to return to the workplace after his retirement: "Come for a visit; let us know how retirement is." The retiree may in turn resolve to return. The invitations and responses are genuine, in the sense that they genuinely express that moment's feelings of loyalty, affection, and regret at the impending separation. Yet they are largely a friendly fiction. Visits from an outsider, which is what the retiree becomes, interrupt the workday. And most work relationships, once they have been severed by retirement, are without much basis for further interchange.

Mrs. Alvarez, who had worked as head of her firm's bookkeeping office, told her coworkers at her retirement party that of course she would return to say hello. Her boss joked that he would call on her regularly to come in and straighten out the books. A year later, Mrs. Alvarez had not visited her former firm, and her former boss had not called her.

Just three of our respondents visited their workplace after their retirement. Two had an ongoing interest in the work being done: a scientist who had headed a research team returned a couple of times in his first year of retirement to talk with former subordinates about new developments in their work, and a former project director in the operating division of a firm became a consultant to the firm's long-range planning group and sometimes dropped in to talk with former coworkers. Only one respondent, Mr. Trexler, a former laboratory technician, visited former coworkers purely as sociability. His experience illustrates why returning to make such visits is unusual.

Mr. Trexler had been pressed to retire by his boss because she believed him to be untrained for his assignments. Not long after his retirement, his boss also left the firm. When we talked with Mr. Trexler two years after his retirement, he had returned to see his former coworkers several times.

I've been going into the company off and on. Every two or three months I go back, say hello to the people, because I like all the people there. They're a marvelous group of people. They treated me good and I appreciated them. We had a lot of nice times together. That was part of my life for forty-three, forty-four years.

The receptionist had known Mr. Trexler for years and greeted him pleasantly, although she apparently kept their interchange brief.

It's a nice, warm feeling when you go in there. The receptionist is a person that's been there for twenty years. She says, "Oh, nice to see you." "Nice to see you again." And you stay there for a couple of minutes, reminisce about some of the people that are there that she knows. So you bring yourself up to date on how things are.

After leaving the receptionist, Mr. Trexler proceeded to his former department. Other firms might not permit a retired employee such easy access, but Mr. Trexler's did.

I go down to my department and I visit the people that I worked with down there in the labs. And of course they're busy on research and development. But it's good to see them. It's, "Well, what the hell are you doing here?" You know, "Back again?" "Well, I like you guys." It's a lot of comedy. And they're a good group of people.

The greeting "What the hell are you doing here?" was not only an affectionate mock challenge but also an expression of a reality: Mr. Trexler no longer belonged in that workplace. Perhaps Mr. Trexler was right not to take its message seriously. But not everyone would willingly subject themselves to this sort of kidding.

A returning retiree can expect to encounter the situation that Mr. Trexler encountered: although former coworkers may be pleased to see him, they are likely soon to be impatient to return to their work. And if entrance to the firm should be guarded by a receptionist hired after the retiree's departure, the retiree's appearance may be greeted with that query that is also a challenge to outsiders: "Can I help you?" In truth, the retiree no longer belongs.

Several respondents maintained a friendly relationship with one or two former coworkers for a time. Yet the longer they were away from the work community, the less they had to share with the former coworkers. They were cut off from company gossip and so knew less and less about developments within their former firms. Unless some new basis for the relationships developed, the relationships were likely to fade.

Identity

In many ways working helps establish people's understanding of themselves. By recognizing their ability to be productive, to make a difference, they assure themselves of their competence and their worth. They are people worthy of their own respect.

Mrs. Allen had run a small contracting business with her husband until her husband's death. She handled the office; he supervised the work. After her husband's death she brought in her older son, a man in his thirties, to be the outside person. Four years later she gave the entire business to the son and retired. The retirement immediately removed her daily list of things to be done. The result was a change in her feelings about herself—a change she did not like.

Sorting things out every day, what's first on the list, what's last on the list, what's the most important thing to do, I got to get this done today – I don't have that daily requirement. I can get up in the morning and I can do this, that, or the other thing. But after being sort of in the harness, you feel kind of like a dilettante of some sort. And I don't like to feel like a dilettante.

The work also helps make us interesting to others. We have stories to tell about how things are done in our sector of the world. Mrs. Chalmers, a former editor, had not especially wanted to retire, but did so after going on disability leave because of work stress. It may have been only she who believed that retirement made her uninteresting to others, but that belief expressed a change in her sense of who she was.

The fact that I had a job and did well in it gave me a credential which I now lack in retirement. I'm not an editor now. I sit and do puzzles at home. Now, that may be interesting – keep it up, it'll keep you out of the poolroom – but it's not something that we want to invite you to come and speak to our group about.

What one does is often used by others as a clue to the sort of person one is. We believe that occupation tells us a fair amount about character. Learning that someone is an engineer suggests to us that he or she is likely careful, ingenious, and constructive. The same goes for learning that someone is a physician or a plumber. But if occupation offers to others hints to our character, it offers the same hints to us. The kind of person we understand ourselves to be is based, in part, on the answer we hear ourselves give to the question "What do you do?"

We also establish social place in part on the basis of occupation. We carry in our minds a map of occupational ratings, and though we do not believe that judges uniformly deserve respect whereas restaurant dishwashers deserve disdain, we will be more deferential to the former. Retirement does not entirely dissipate the respect associated with a former status, but it does weaken it. The occupational self-description "I used to be a physician, but I'm retired now" may do well enough to elicit respect, but it will not do nearly as well as "I'm a physician."

The membership in a community of work that occupation provides can become part of one's understanding of self. In some occupations having a place in a particular organization or institution may be as important as the work actually performed. Managers and administrators, if asked what they do, would be likely to respond not only with a job title but also with the name of their firm: "I'm a vice president of the X Corporation." Being a bank employee, or an employee of a respected university, irrespective of what one does, can contribute to self-esteem.

Finally, except for the self-employed who work out of their homes, work provides a place to go: an office, a laboratory bench, a desk, that can be made one's own. Removing personal items from what had long been one's own space can be one of the hardest aspects of retiring.

In our interview with Dr. Metcalf, the research scientist, a couple of months after his retirement, we asked him whether retirement made things different. He did his best to convey what it felt like to undergo identity change as a consequence of retirement. First, he was no longer the person who did experimental science. His work had been taken from him.

I don't know whether I can put it into words, because it's a new feeling. I haven't developed a description of it. It's sort of a vague feeling of unease, I guess, not easy to define. I am no longer doing something I was trained to do and spent thirty-odd years doing. I'm not using my basic skills as a scientist, as an experimental scientist. The mechanical skills, the mental skills—designing experiments, interpreting results, all that sort of thing, which is what a scientist does—I'm no longer doing that. And there's a certain funny feeling. It's strange.

I'm still sort of feeling my way into this. A new emotion takes a long while before you can really define what you mean by it. This is sort of a vague feeling of discontinuity—suddenly not doing something that I've been doing eight hours a day for thirty-five years.

I'm not unhappy. I don't know what sort of analogy I can give to this, but in a way it's rather as though you've been crippled. You've been working all your life doing this job; you're no longer doing it. It's as though you had some major disability, a physical disability, that stops you from doing what you used to do.

Dr. Metcalf was describing the experience of identity change when he talked of a new feeling, a vague feeling of unease. It is the feeling of not being who one was, of having to reconceptualize oneself. It is triggered by recognizing that you no longer do what you once did, that you no longer have the office or laboratory you once had, that you no longer have the same meaning to others. You may begin to suspect that whatever had been required to be that person—energy or steadfastness or intelligence or responsiveness—has been lost.

But identity change entails still more. Dr. Metcalf felt that he no longer belonged where he had when he was working and that he possibly—he did not find the thought welcome—had become a member of a community of old men.

It's a big transition from working ten-hour days, figuring out problems and that sort of thing, to having all my time to myself. It's a big switch. I'm starting to work on things to do, but it's going to take a while for me to adjust to it.

You no longer feel you're in the mainstream of things. This morning I went out to the square to get some coffee, and I take a bus when I do that, and I was standing at the bus stop and all these old men were wandering around. I thought, My God, I'm part of this community now! You know, I'm beginning to be part of this group! It was a funny feeling.

Hanging onto part of what had supported one's identity can reduce the shock of total loss of the preretirement identity. Former identities can be maintained, at least partially, by keeping one's former office or former title or by finding occasions to display what had been one's occupational skills. Academics often can retain an office at their university despite retirement and can sometimes continue to work with students. Retired physicians retain their licenses to practice. Four of the five retired physicians in our sample found a way to continue to practice part time: in a college clinic, as an adviser to a health program, as a medical examiner in a military induction center, and by seeing a few patients at home. The one who did not practice part time attended medical lectures at a hospital in his neighborhood. Although it is more difficult for a retired businessman to retain an occupational identity, some manage by acting as consultants or by serving on the boards of arts organizations or charities.

Even so, it is not possible to retire without identity change. The many retirees whose feelings of worth had been sustained by their occupations may discover that retirement fosters feelings of nostalgia for who they once were.

Gains in Retirement

The losses in retirement of community, structure, and identity are real. Yet most of those who voluntarily retire find that retirement's gains outweigh its losses. Chief among the gains are retirement's freedom from the many stresses of work. In addition, there is freedom from the obligations that work had imposed and the accompanying freedom to use one's time as one wishes.

Many retirees report that the most important benefit of retirement is that it freed them from work stress. Some retirees had developed ulcers or migraines or insomnia and had been advised to reduce the stress in their lives. Some, before their retirement, had experienced angina or heart attacks and had been warned by their physicians that they were courting death by continuing to subject themselves to stress. Two of our respondents said they thought that retirement had saved their lives.

Work is regularly stressful: a boss wants a difficult task performed; a misunderstanding occurs with a colleague; a job is not going well; a client has a complaint. Coworkers can compete for recognition, perks, or one's job. All of these lead to mobilization, high alertness, and a state of tension. When mobilization persists, the consequence is wear and tear on the body. In many jobs the threat of potential failure, with consequent reprimand and humiliation, provokes just such persisting mobilization. Its expressions include preoccupation and irritability, away from work as well as on the job. There may well be nights in which worry over work interrupts sleep.

Retirees who had been subject to job stress believed that it had made them less satisfactory as parents and spouses. They had missed family celebrations and school graduations. They were preoccupied through the evening, and if the spouse or the children wanted their attention they became irritable. They did not want to talk about their troubles at work and they had not been able to think about much else.

Mr. Hindes, who had been a service manager in a public utility, was among respondents for whom the major benefit of retirement was escape from work stress.

All those years of pressure and stress, fighting to keep a position, somebody always breathing down your neck looking for your job, or the next boss coming in and not liking you. Or politics being involved, and it was really not what you could do or what you had done. The whole story was: "OK, that was yesterday. What have you done for me today?" Now I sit back and I figure I have a pension, I have Social Security—I still have things that I have to do, but not under the same stress.

Mr. Mathers, the former sales manager, was among those who had experienced a serious heart attack and was told he was putting himself at risk if he did not slow down. When he did finally retire, he said that the retirement was pure blessing. He was no longer under stress:

I've only been home for a week and a couple of days but I really enjoy it. I can sleep a little later. Not that I do—I think the latest I've slept was about quarter of nine—but lately my routine has been maybe six o'clock or six-fifteen or six-thirty, and for many years it was five-thirty and I was out of the house by six. I find it very nice, really.

Not having the pressure of work feels wonderful. It really does. I feel relaxed. I feel at ease. I can honestly sit down at night and say to myself, gee, I don't have to confront that traffic in the morning. I don't have to be concerned about orders. I don't have to be concerned about somebody didn't get their products, or the trucks didn't get out. It's a weight off my shoulders.

A year after his retirement Mr. Mathers reiterated that retirement was turning out to be a blessing. He was grateful that he now had time for increased companionship with his wife and with others in his family. And he continued to be pleased that he no longer was beset by the demands of the job.

It's been an opportunity to spend more time with my wife, particularly, and my children and my mother, who is living with us now. She's ninety-two years of age and she's been living with us. I have more time to spend with them. And I've had more time to pursue some of the things that I've always wanted to do — pick up around the house and do a little bit of work in the house and do a little bit of reading. And just relaxing quite a bit.

The job was very strain-filled and it really took a lot out of me. I had a tremendous amount of responsibility. And I just feel as if a great weight has been relieved from me. I feel very good about it, really.

Two years after his retirement Mr. Mathers made the same assessment. He also noted that the job stress had been endangering:

When I was working, I was constantly on the go. Constantly. The retirement in my case has been beneficial because at the pace I was going, I was endangering my health.

It was an awesome responsibility because in a certain sense I had the livelihood of a lot of people in my hands. And I could never release myself. I could be sitting and talking to my children or my wife or having a cup of tea with my wife, and my thoughts were always about what was going on in the company. Now I'm completely relieved of that.

For a time just after his retirement Mr. Mathers had encouraged his former subordinates to telephone him to talk about what was going on in the firm. Gradually the calling slowed. By a year after his retirement Mr. Mathers hardly heard from any of the men who had reported to him, and by two years after retirement he no longer heard from them at all. Now and then he still thought of the company and wondered how it was doing. But he had no desire to call anyone to find out. He was pleased to be retired.

Some prospective retirees worry that they will miss job stress once they retire. They witness themselves dealing well with crises and think of the stress as energizing them. Mr. Reynolds, a division director, was among those who worried that he would miss work's stresses. Before his retirement, he had said:

I gave many years to the company and never regretted it, never regretted a single day. There's no question in my mind that after I retire I may miss a lot of the stress, the pressures that go on every single day. People miss things that they're doing. I think I'll miss the running around and trying to meet schedules and see projects get completed, see something that you worked on completed and in service and operating.

But when we talked with Mr. Reynolds eighteen months after his retirement, he was pleased by the disappearance of what he now recognized as having been chronic stress.

I don't have to get up in the morning and shave and look at myself in the mirror and say, My God, what do I have to do today? All these things that by a certain time I have to finish—I have a performance evaluation to make, things like that—there's nothing like that now. I feel relieved. It's great.

When he worked, Mr. Reynolds's life may have possessed excitements that his retirement lacked. But Mr. Reynolds enjoyed his time with friends, children, and grandchildren. He traveled a bit. He still kept an appointment book, but now it contained only such entries as dinner times with friends, visits from the children, and the occasional medical appointment. He did not mind having slowed down.

Retirement's second great contribution, after its relief from work stress, is its ending of work's constraints. Retirement means not having to be at work at a particular time and not having to give a block of time to the tasks of the job.

Retirement means not having to set aside evening time to think through issues from the day's work or to prepare for the work of tomorrow. During one's work years, sleeping late is a luxury available only on weekends and holidays. In retirement it is possible every day. The commute to and from the office is a thing of the past. Because it is not necessary to get up early for work, it becomes possible to stay up late the night before to watch television or to read a novel or to play bridge with friends.

Although it may take effort to avoid slipping into a lax and pointless day, most retirees focus on the freedom rather than on whatever problems there may be in its use.[6] Dr. Metcalf, the former research scientist, was among respondents who could see both sides. The positive implications of the freedom appeared to matter more to him, however—and in this he was typical.

The freedom has to be dealt with. And it's not easy. I've been used to a structured environment. Now it's unstructured. And I probably need a structured environment to function well. On the other hand, say that it's ten degrees below and you're starting out of the house. I don't need to go out today! And you feel happy. And that's a marvelous feeling. That's part of the freedom.

The freedom of retirement is not only a freedom from the need to respond to work's demands. It is also, notably, the freedom to engage in new activities, thoughts, and experiences.

The extraordinary nature of this "freedom to" warrants contemplation. Retirement makes available the freedom to do just about anything, health and income permitting: travel, of course; the development of new skills; contribution to one's community; time with the grandchildren. All of this can be undertaken at one's own pace. Not since adolescence will there have been comparable opportunity to choose one's activities and to organize one's time free from obligations and responsibilities. Retirement is an extraordinary period in one's life.

As they contemplate what they might do with their time, retirees have the usual two risks of planning. On one hand, they risk venturing too little and later regretting that they failed to take the trip they had promised themselves or the return to a musical instrument they had once played. On the other hand, they risk venturing too much— for example, franchising a business for which they lack background or time or financing. But in our sample, at least, it seemed that few ventured too much and that even among those who ventured little, absent money worries and social isolation (discussed in the following chapters), retirement can be a good time in one's life.

Retirement as a Milestone

Quite apart from the gains and losses associated with leaving work, retirement has meaning as a milestone. It signals the beginning of a phase of life that had for a very long time been out in the future, perhaps only half believed in. Although one had known throughout one's working life that retirement was located somewhere in the future, it is likely to have seemed far off almost until it was about to happen.

Once one enters retirement, the years of one's working life—indeed, of one's entire life—can seem to have sped by. One's career seems oddly telescoped, with the early years vivid, as though they had happened only recently, the intermediate years a blur, and the recent past again vivid and, seemingly, not so very far from the days of starting out.

Mr. Ulrich, the former project director for a financial institution, discussed finding himself at an age at which his career had ended:

I have disbelief in my age. I just can't believe it. You know, it's not possible that it can end. After all, thirty-eight years.

Mr. Ulrich's thoughts went on to what might be the next milestone after retirement—the ending of life. That had seemed no more real than retirement had seemed a few years earlier and yet now it was clearly out there, somewhere in the future, just as retirement had once been:

And of course, you run into this, this has nothing to do with retirement, the fact that your life is coming to a close. There's the specter of death. I'm sixty-five; how many more years do I have? When you're forty, you're never going to die. Not that I have a terrible fear of that; it's just that retirement is an indication that I may be retiring from life.

Let's face it, when one retires, one is saying one has entered the final phase of life. This is it. There is no more after this. What I mean is, you are going to die. I'm not brooding about it. But you are walking down the last corridor, whatever. And it may be wonderful, but it is still the last one. There's no phase after that. That's it.

I'm not particularly afraid of dying. On the other hand, I'd like to see my grandchildren grow up. So it's sad. You're going to leave, to shuffle off this mortal coil.

The same awareness that the end of life was nearing was expressed by Mrs. Graham, a former editor. Mrs. Graham was not especially given to rumination but could not help noting that she did not have a great many years left.

You know perfectly well your whole life that life ends. But when you're twenty, you say: I'm going to live to be a hundred and I'm not going to worry about it.

When you're sixty, you think: Well, I'm probably not going to live to be a hundred, and so that means I only have maybe twenty more years to live. Maybe I only have fifteen. You get to a certain age and you know that there is no possibility that you're going to live fifty more years.

Most retirees preferred not to dwell on issues of mortality. Enough to acknowledge that somewhere down the road, though they could hope still years away, were the final milestones of frailty and death. On the other hand, retirement encouraged many retirees to consider how well they had done in their lives. Their criteria differed, but the retirees frequently cited a nice way of life, success at work, and children doing well. As they looked back, retirees who felt that their achievements had fallen short of what they wished they had been, or that their family lives had not gone as well as they might have, tried to reconcile themselves to their regret. Mr. Trexler, the former technician, was among those pleased with how well his children were doing, and that mattered a lot to him, but he felt he had not done as much in his work or in his life as he could have, and that made his retirement bittersweet:

I felt as though I should have done more in my life, more than I did. Not being as bright as the next guy, I felt as though maybe I missed a lot in life. But there again, my life has gone by. I didn't really plan on retirement. If I did think more about retirement and so forth—and a lot of other things—I would have achieved a lot more in life.

Most of our respondents did little planning for whatever might follow the life phase of retirement. When we asked what thoughts they had regarding the more distant future, we might be told of a desire to avoid a nursing home or dependence on relatives. Beyond that, there seemed not much to be said.

Few retirees in our sample felt that retirement meant they were old. True, the calendar had flipped enough times to justify the retirement, and it was possible that one or two signs of aging had crept up on them, but they nevertheless felt themselves to be the same people they had always been, with the same energy, or only a bit less, and now with new freedom.

Chapter Four

Money

Before their retirement our respondents, like others soon to retire from middle-income occupations, generally could estimate their retirement income by adding together their anticipated pension income with the income they would receive from stocks, bonds, and property.[1] They could be fairly sure that things would work financially. But until they saw what would happen, they could not be certain. One example was Mr. Paige, the computer engineer, who described his thoughts as he tried to plan an orderly retirement:

As near as I can come up with the numbers, I think we are going to be all right. I think we are probably going to be very close. I get a pension from the place I retired from; I get a small pension from a place I worked before that; my wife gets a pension from the Department of Education. I *think* it is going to work.

The problem that our respondents encountered derived from the way they had managed their finances during their working lives. Rather than rely on budgets, most of them had decided the level of spending they could afford by seeing what had happened over the previous pay period. If they were paid monthly, then at the end of each month they would check to see if money was left. If money had run out, they would have to tighten up. If money had been left over, they could loosen. If the money just made it to the end of the pay period, there was no need to make changes but tension could arise over spending in the current month. And since expenditures tend to rise to the level of resources, this was by no means an unusual development. Mr. Ulrich described it as swimming from island to island and just barely making it. But for thirty-eight years, in his case, he did make it. Month-to-month recalibration worked.

This did not mean that the soon-to-retire did not try to calculate whether their retirement income would cover their expenditures. Some drew up one budget after another. But they did not trust their conclusions. Before his retirement Mr. Ulrich said:

It takes a lot of guts to retire, in my opinion. It's an unknown. You can say, well, the pension will be this much, the Social Security will be that much, and then you compare that to your expenses and there's always some leeway. And you know damn well, if you've ever budgeted, that you can budget 'til hell freezes over, and you're never going to budget correctly. You're always going to spend more than you budget for. And that's part of the frightening aspect of retirement. You know that you're going to spend more.

Mr. Paige, like Mr. Ulrich, had managed without a budget when he was working. His way of assessing how he was doing had been to check at the end of the year whether he was putting money away or losing ground.

I really haven't got a financial plan. I didn't know what we spent when I was working, except that we never had much money left over at the end of the year, apparently. We never had a budget as such. We never really needed one. We have always come out at least even by the end of the year.

Even when people try to budget, they judge how well they are doing by matching their actual income to their actual expenditures. Retirement will present a new situation, in which there will be a different income and a different set of expenditures. Guessing how well they will match is not easy.

Almost always, income will be reduced: retirement income tends to be between half and two-thirds of income during employment.[2] But whether this will affect the quality of life depends on expenditures.

And most retirees are uncertain about what their retirement expenditures will be. They can make guesses, but they will not feel confident until they have at least a few months of experience. Mr. Paige wanted to be retired for a year before deciding how well he was doing financially.

What it is going to be in retirement, I don't know. I have everything all written down as to what we had at the beginning of the year when I retired—what is in the savings account, what is in the checking account, what is in the IRA, the 401(k). And twelve months from now I'll go and add it up again and see whether we are ahead or not, see if we break even, or how far behind we are. Until I know that, I don't know how I could plan ahead, because while I did sit down and add up a lot of numbers and make a lot of calculations, I don't know if it is going to work or not, because I don't know what we are going to be spending.

As far as next year, I don't know—more of the same if I'm not going up a wall. And if I am going up the wall, I've made the mental commitment, maybe I'll work part time.

Presumably if Mr. Paige saw himself losing ground financially, he could lower his standard of living. But like most retirees, he was determined to maintain the standard of living he had established when he was working.[3] He believed that his wife shared that concern as she thought about their joint retirement.

My wife has stated that she wants the same lifestyle in retirement as we had before. The retirement question was: Are we going to be able to maintain what we are doing now? I think that was my wife's main angle. And I hear her and I think she is right.

What does it mean to "maintain what we are doing now"? It means more than having a particular quality of food, clothing, and shelter. A reasonable assessment is that it means being able to maintain the consumption style of one's friends and neighbors. Retirees want an income good enough to enable them to remain in their homes, continue to see movies and go out to dinner, if that is what the people they know do, and, within reason, afford the kind of travel enjoyed by the people they know. Mr. Paige spoke of the many people with whom he had discussed his retirement plans. He would have been distressed if retirement meant he would have to begin scrimping in a way they did not.

Mr. Paige was fairly confident that his retirement would go well, but he had some apprehension: "There may be a problem at the end of the year that we have enough money to do all these things, to keep the same lifestyle." Until he saw how retirement worked, he could not be sure.

Many retirees had pension plans that required that they make a number of decisions at the time they elected to receive payments: Lump sum or regular monthly check? Spouse coverage should you die? What sort of health plan coverage? They found themselves perplexed. How could they work out the options that would best fit an unknown future? Professor Janelle, who taught humanities at the undergraduate and graduate school level, described the experience:

There're about five or six options that you have to make, all these decisions, before you draw on your income. And I never realized it. I always thought naively that you just pay in and then you get something back. You have to decide whether you want ten years guaranteed, fifteen years guaranteed, twenty years guaranteed, a half to your survivor, two-thirds to your survivor, nothing to the survivor. You can have one lump sum. It's a long range of options. And once you make a decision how you get your money and what you want, you can never change it anymore.

I attended some seminars. They only were more confusing. I have oodles of material. And they send you projections. They calculate, if you do this and that, how much you'd get monthly. And then you can roll over a stock fund into a bond fund. And they say it's better to have a sure income than the gamble with the stock market.

Is it better to have a higher monthly pension payment or to insure that one's spouse has income should one die first? How can anyone know? Either decision might be mistaken.[4]

Retirement ushers in a new way of life. Employment, the main source of retirees' income throughout their adult lives, will end. What the retirees will have in its place is a set of untested income sources:

perhaps a pension provided by their firms, which they may believe in but have not yet seen; Social Security, which they also have not yet received; their savings, which they have spent their lives trying to augment and now may have to deplete; for some, investments, which can be solid but are vulnerable to losses; and property. Property, of all these, may be the most nearly tangible, and owning something that people want to rent can be reassuring. But having to rely for the years to come only on what already has been set aside is like sailing off into a sea whose placidity may be temporary, with provisions likely to be perishable and no knowledge of the length of the voyage.[5] Even those retirees who had so much in savings, investments, and pension that there was little likelihood of their ever being in need could become uneasy when they thought about no longer being able to earn.

Mrs. Edwards, a widow, talked with us about her decision to retire from her position as an agency executive. Her savings and promised pension appeared adequate. In addition, she owned her own home and had property in a vacation area. She should have felt utterly secure. And yet the future was unknowable; anything could happen.

I feel very fortunate in that I could manage retirement since I own a house and I have additional income and so on, although certainly it will not provide a very lavish kind of life. But then you worry about the unexpected illness or a lot of other things which can throw a monkey wrench into everything in terms of what you saved and what you've tried to hang on to.

I guess you can never feel secure, no matter what you've accumulated. No matter if you feel you've got potentially a reasonably comfortable income for the rest of your life, there's still not a sense of security about that because one thing can happen that can destroy it all. Were I to need help in the house, help maintaining myself, it would really be a drain. And it would exhaust a lot of resources.

Nor is it much of a comfort to have children who might help. Mrs. Edwards, who had two children, could have thought of them as people to whom she could turn for help should her own resources fail. But the children were just starting their own adulthoods, and she wanted to be able to help them rather than have to ask them help her. There might someday be grandchildren for her to help as well. She did not want, ever, to be dependent on her children.

I have a couple of kids that could still use some help and so I think of that. And, hopefully, someday I'll have some grandchildren who I might want to help. And then, of course, most people will say they don't want to be dependent on their children, ever.

Several of our respondents who received lump sums on retiring were uncertain of their ability to actively manage the funds. There was great variation here. Some respondents felt entirely confident of their ability to make wise investment decisions. A few gave a great deal of time to reading investment publications and to following the market. But more had never given investments much attention, not even during the stock bubble of the nineties: they were perplexed by having to invest retirement funds.

Mr. Evans had been a field engineer for a utility. Just before his retirement, he had lost five thousand dollars in the mutual fund in which he had invested his retirement funds. He removed the remainder of the money. He also chose to take as much of his other retirement moneys as he could as a lump sum.

I just lost through no fault of my own almost five thousand dollars. In the pension plan we had, you have a mutual fund; they can be changed at quarters of the year. In the process of retiring, all this stuff is being shuffled around and changed, and the last statement compared to the quarter before that, there was about five grand involved. From one statement to another, it just disappeared.

On retiring I went to see a tax man I have because I had to make some decisions as to whether I wanted the company to invest my money and give me an increased pension or whether I would take a lump sum and put it somewhere else. Well, from everything I was able to find out, my options were to take the lump sum and put it into an annuity because it would pay me a much better rate.

But I don't want to fool around with that kind of money, because I don't have the knowledge and I don't want to lose it. So I have to go by where I can get the information. I can talk to people I know who have made investments, people who are working their money a little bit. A lot of them are working it through CDs.

And then, there's an annuity; basically it's a CD but they give you a little better rate of interest on it. And whether I would want to go in that direction, I don't know. But, see, the point is, you can make a good investment but you also tie up your money. And that I don't want to do, because if I need to liquefy any, I got to have it. You want it now. And I don't want to be penalized for taking my own money.

So you say okay, I've got X amount of dollars, I can put this into this and possibly get this out of it. So my best bet is like CDs or just a straight bank account or these annuities. The CDs sound good because you can do a three months or six months situation. But the rates are so low now, it's hardly worth it. I can put it in the bank for that.

So I'm going to play around with this and get the best deal I can get and still be able to do what I want to do. A lot of it is a wait and see proposition. And you're a little leery anyway, because I have never been in a situation where I was in the market other than through work. And so I don't have the knowledge to play with the stock market or to play with a lot of the things that the market does.

Several respondents turned to financial advisers for help. Their choice of advisers seemed haphazard: if an accountant had helped them with taxes, they might ask him for investment advice, or they might consult a financial adviser who had given a presentation at their firm. They might, as Mr. Evans did, incorporate the advice into their obsessing over the best course to follow, or they might simply follow the advice they were given, without completely trusting it.[6]

Mr. Hindes, like Mr. Evans, had retired with substantial savings. Mr. Hindes had also been employed by a public utility, although he had been part of its bureaucracy rather than in the field. Like Mr. Evans, he did not trust himself to invest his savings. Unlike Mr. Evans, he engaged an investment firm. The firm was one from which he had received flyers; otherwise he knew nothing about the firm. He nevertheless gave the company authority to manage everything he had.

I have a financial adviser. When I left work, they were sending bulletins around, looking for business, so I took them up on it. And I ended up rolling over my savings and everything else into this investment outfit. And they kind of take care. They send me statements monthly and then they send me statements quarterly.

I just got some statements yesterday. I have books and I kind of watch what's happening with the investments. I can check and see how things are doing. Now there's some things I don't like, what I saw when I was looking at them yesterday, and I'm planning to call the representative and ask a few questions on what's happening. Why is the stock falling and why are my investments going down?

You have to watch the people that are supposed to be doing things because they're making their daily bread by sales. Buy and sell, they're getting their commissions. And they could care less what happens to you. So you got to watch it. But these fellows that I have been talking to seem to be very good.

Yet despite retirees' initial apprehensions and their opportunities for missteps, financial life in retirement ordinarily goes well, at least in the first years of retirement. Surveys have found that the great majority of retired people, once they have some experience with their income and expenditures, are satisfied with their financial situations.[7]

Life in retirement does cost less than life at work.[8] Transportation costs are reduced, business clothes no longer need be bought, and lunch can be eaten at home. Social Security taxes end. It is no longer necessary to put aside income for retirement, although continued saving might be a good idea during retirement's early years. Children are no longer dependents, with perhaps the exception of a child finishing the final years of his or her education. For many respondents, the lower cost of life in retirement was a surprise.

Mr. Williams, formerly a partner in a family business, had made up a budget before his retirement to judge whether he could afford retirement. He said:

Before I understood retirement, I did a budget and I anticipated my expenses would remain constant. I have a brother who retired at age fifty-five; he's been retired now thirteen years, and he said my budget was crazy because you don't spend anywhere near as much money when you're retired as you do when you're working. And I wasn't convinced of it. But he was right. I haven't bought a shirt; I haven't bought any suits. What would I do with the suits that I have in the closet? My wife has still bought dresses, and I may need some neckties. But no, you don't spend as much money.

Satisfaction with the financial situation of retirement seems primarily to have stemmed from retirees' experience as they monitored what was left after their bills were paid. Generally, they found they were managing well enough.

Most of our respondents owned their own homes, with paid-up mortgages. Many had bought their homes years earlier for prices that now seemed amazingly low. The increase in housing prices had since turned the homes into substantial stores of value. The retirees could reassure themselves that if they ran into real financial trouble, they could mortgage or sell the homes.

Among our respondents there appeared little correlation between being satisfied with retirement income and the level of that income. We found, as have those surveying the general population, that low-income retirees were nearly as satisfied with their incomes as were people whose retirement incomes were comparatively high.[9]

To see how this comes about, consider the assessments of their financial situations made by two respondents whose postretirement financial circumstances differed markedly. The first is a former professor whose pension income was about three times the pension income of the second, a former college janitor. The former professor, in addition, had savings and investments on which he could draw should he ever need to. The former janitor had neither. Each was satisfied with his retirement income; indeed, the former janitor may have been a bit more satisfied.

Professor Rembow prided himself on having given little attention to his income during his working life. Nor did he have much apprehension about managing in retirement. Indeed, he thought his income would go up in retirement because the end of teaching responsibility would give him time for consulting and public speaking. Things did not turn out that way, but nevertheless his retirement income was perfectly adequate.

All my life I earned enough, or we earned enough, that we were comfortable. So it seemed like a terrible waste of useful time to worry whether I could get an additional tenth of a percent in interest and whether this stock or this CD was more effective than another. I just spent very little time on the accumulation of whatever wealth I made. I really paid relatively little attention to investment.

I expected when I retired that my income would shoot up, between retirement income and what I would be earning. That part has not materialized. Now I don't have the sense that I can always earn. I've earned a little bit in honoraria, but the sense that I can always go out and earn an honorarium or something like that is no longer quite there. I haven't actively sought consulting jobs, and they haven't come.

In retirement Professor Rembow did give attention to his financial situation, a change from his practice during his career. But he tried not to let concern about finances limit what he did.

I look in the stock pages more frequently. I should add that we inherited a little bit when my wife's parents and my mother died, so there's a little bit more to look at. But I do not play the market. I do not have an investment adviser. I don't study advisory services religiously. I'm not about to regret that if I only had had the sense to do such and such, that the five thousand dollars could now be ten and instead they're five. So be it.

I'm comfortable and I don't have to let money sour my life. In the match between investing and thinking about future professional activities, the professional activities win out, hands down. I couldn't think of saying no, I can't do that.

Professor Rembow did not keep a budget. He decided how well he was doing by checking on how much money he had left after his bills were paid. He was pleasantly surprised to discover that he was doing well.

I have noticed a difference in our disposable income within the last few years. Since our youngest son finished college—graduate school, actually; he got his degree only in January—we have more money to put into savings each month than we did before.

Professor Rembow was confident that his savings would last beyond his lifetime and his wife's lifetime. He had begun to think about what he would leave his children and grandchildren.

I have given a little bit more attention to inheritance, to our leaving resources to our children. And now that our first grandchild is coming, some sense of assuring his or her education, with university costs now ranging over a hundred thousand dollars for four years, is certainly a part of my thinking. Those are things that I've given a little more thought to.

If Professor Rembow had run into financial problems because his income and savings had not covered his bills, perhaps because of an unexpected illness, he might have given more energy to finding paid work or might have tried to cut back on expenditures. But since he had not run into problems, he could feel that his financial situation was satisfactory.

Now let us turn to Mr. Harris, the former college janitor. Mr. Harris fell into our sample because he rented an apartment in one of the middle-income suburbs from which we drew the sample. His college pension, together with his Social Security payments, amounted to only twenty-one thousand dollars in 1999. Nevertheless, Mr. Harris was content with his financial situation—indeed, quite pleased.

To be honest with you, I'm doing better retired than when I was working. I don't need anything. I got everything here—what I need, what I want. And with me not smoking, not drinking, I don't have that many expenses. In fact, I have very little expenses. I'm a homebody—very seldom will I go out at night.

Much more than did Professor Rembow, Mr. Harris kept track of expenditures. But like Professor Rembow, Mr. Harris decided how well he was doing by seeing how much money he had left at the end of the month, after all his bills were paid. Mr. Harris thought he was doing well.

I have a book—an accounting book is exactly what it is—and every bill that I pay every month I have it all written down. The gas and all the other bills come in like within the first twelve days of the month. The rent—I'm lucky; the landlady only charges me seven hundred dollars—the telephone bill and all the other bills are in by usually the fifteenth of the month. So I know exactly what is going out that month mostly by the fifteenth. The only bill that comes in later in the month is the light bill.

I know exactly how much I have in the checking account each month and how much I allow for myself. I usually set aside in the checking account – I figured this all out – like two or three hundred dollars for myself a month. Sometimes you go over; you borrow it from months you don't go over. But you set yourself on that amount. And, as I said, I'm just a homebody; I really don't do that much.

I've been able to save more than when I was working because when you're working you're always doing something. This way you know that now that you're retired, you're on a set income, and you've got to sit down and figure things out.

Mr. Harris practiced small economies. He had a good friend who joined him in the evening a few times a week and shared the cost of dinner. In the winter, to save on heating, he closed off his front room except for the couple of hours in the evening when he watched television. Although he owned a pickup truck, he mostly kept it parked except for a day a week when he would use his truck to transport food to his church's Open Pantry. Once in a while minor ailments led him to visit a veterans hospital in a distant suburb; he then took public transportation.

Mr. Harris had an active social life, much of it centered on his church. The church was only a couple of blocks from his home, making it easy for him to get there. On Sundays he served as an usher; on other days he worked with the church's ministry to the poor. In addition, he valued his relationship with the friend with whom he frequently spent evenings; was on good terms with his landlady, whom he advised on tax returns; and on occasion used the truck to drive a neighbor to a medical appointment. He had a good many relatives in the area, although he was the last of the siblings. He kept up with several nephews, nieces, and cousins by telephone. On Sundays, after church, he walked to a cousin's home, where he had Sunday dinner. During evenings when he was alone, he watched television—in the summer, major league baseball. He was, in all, content with life.

Only two of our respondents actually experienced serious financial problems in the interval during which we were in touch with them. In each case family medical expenses were the reason: in one case the medical expenses of the respondent's mother; in the other, the respondent's wife.

The first case involved the mother of Mrs. Pierce, the former marketing manager who had moved from a disability leave to retirement. Expenses for her own illness were small and were covered by health insurance. On the other hand, expenses for Mrs. Pierce's mother were sizable. Mrs. Pierce's mother had experienced a disabling stroke and needed almost constant care. Medicare paid for her medical treatment, but it was up to Mrs. Pierce and her husband to pay for her nursing. Mrs. Pierce told us, rather mournfully, "No matter how much you put aside, no matter how much you prepare for it, you may have to use that retirement money, if you are so willing, to help care for someone else in the family."

Mrs. Pierce's husband had retired early because of a damaged hip, a memento of football playing days. His retirement income was fairly low, but the two pensions together—his and his wife's—would have been adequate except for the nursing care expenses. Those expenses sent the Pierces into debt.

About a year after Mrs. Pierce's retirement her mother died. The Pierces then discovered that paying down their debt in addition to meeting their other obligations left them broke at the end of the month. When we last saw them, their housing costs were about to increase and they were worried about how they would manage.

The other respondent with serious financial problems in the early days of his retirement was Mr. Eggert, formerly a supervisor in a state agency. Mr. Eggert had retired on a pension that would have been easily enough to maintain his standard of living, especially with the addition of Social Security. But his wife required extensive dental work, most of it not covered by Medicare, as well as psychiatric treatment that was only partially covered by Medicare. Mr. Eggert believed that he would run through his savings within a year. When we last talked with him, he was planning to do tax work part time. If that did not produce enough income, he did not know what he would do.

Respondents who were satisfied with their current incomes could be apprehensive about the future. Their concern was not so great that it produced sleepless nights, but it was significant. They recognized that an illness not covered by insurance or a need for nursing care was always possible. And they worried that Medicare, on which most retirees rely, could not be expected to cover all their expenses.[10]

Mr. Mathers, the former sales manager, had what might have seemed to be adequate financing for the rest of his life. He had taken his pension as a lump sum and put it in certificates of deposit. He had also bought annuities. As much as he could, he avoided using his savings or investments for current expenses, instead covering his monthly bills with his Social Security check and with contributions from the three adult children still living at home. His view of the future was that he would be fine so long as he was not hit by unexpected health care costs. But he was apprehensive: unexpected health costs could happen to anyone.

I've been living off my Social Security primarily. I have three children still at home and they're contributing to the house, which has been quite beneficial. Every once in a while I have to tap into savings. Like we have insurance bills, taxes, and things like that, and I go to the bank and I withdraw. I have been pulling it out of my money market fund.

I haven't touched my certificates of deposit as yet. And I have four annuities. So I feel I don't have any real financial problems. But I don't feel that I am financially secure. Any big, heavy medical bills would put a dent in my money.

Although health care was respondents' primary concern as they tried to look into the future, some respondents, especially those who were more sophisticated financially, also felt uneasy about the effects inflation could have on their fixed incomes. Although Social Security payments and some government pensions are indexed to the cost of living, pensions provided by private employers are almost always for fixed sums.[11]

Mr. Hall, formerly an executive in a consulting firm, had retired with sizable savings and a handsome pension income. He felt he was doing pretty well in retirement.

I've been maintaining about the same income in retirement as before I retired. I won't be able to do this forever, but we could shrink back to some degree without feeling like we were pinched. At the moment I don't see any compelling need to change anything much.

Inflation has been very good since we've retired. Inflation really could change our whole setup. That's a danger we'll have to face if it happens.

There's not a lot you can do to hedge it. We're doing some things, a few things you can do to hedge it. Our investments, about half is fixed income and half isn't.

Another respondent, Mr. Crittenden, had been worried about the adequacy of his pension. Once he had retired, however, he discovered that his retirement income more than covered his expenditures. He was pleased that he could continue to save. He said, only half joking, that his aim now was to be sure of a comfortable nursing home should he and his wife require nursing home care. For Mr. Crittenden and other respondents, reasons for concern seemed ever present.

A Note on Social Security

The Social Security program has been one of the most successful of governmental programs. In 2000, of employed or formerly employed Americans over the age of sixty-five (the great majority formerly employed) fewer than one in ten were below the official poverty line. If Social Security income were subtracted, almost half would have been below the poverty line.[12]

Most of the retired receive Social Security payments: a study of Social Security Administration data for the year 2000 reports that about 90 percent of those sixty-five or older are covered by Social Security.[13] In comparison, only about 60 percent had any savings or investments, and slightly more than 40 percent received private or government pensions. Approximately two-thirds of those who received Social Security payments relied on those payments for at least half their total incomes, and about a third relied on them for at least 90 percent of their total incomes.[14]

Our respondents, all but a few of them retired from middle-class occupations, were as a group better off than the average American. Most had savings and investments in addition to Social Security and, except for those who had been self-employed, most had pensions. For the best-off third of our respondents, our estimate is that Social Security provided no more than a fifth of their income; and for the best off among these, a good deal less. They all could have managed without

Social Security, although they were pleased to have it. But for respondents on a tighter budget, Social Security made the difference between worry and comfort.

None of our respondents was dependent on Social Security alone. Nevertheless, for several Social Security was essential. It provided about half of Mr. Harris's income; without it, he could not possibly have paid his bills.[15]

Chapter Five

Social Isolation

Retirees not only are likely to lose a part of their income with retirement; they also are likely to lose the interactions of the workday. These interactions include the brief greetings from receptionists and people passed in hallways and the brief conversations with coworkers before settling down to the tasks of the day. Interactions of this sort are not meaningless, no matter how little information is exchanged; rather, they affirm that the participants have a place in the work community. They support participants' identities as people who have something to contribute. Augmenting these contacts during the workday might be more substantial encounters, including meetings, consultations, and lunches with others also in the work world, perhaps from other settings. Augmenting them, too, would be a great many incidental encounters during the trip to and from work, most of them with strangers, some with people with whom there might be a nodding acquaintance, such as a security guard or owner of a kiosk where coffee and a newspaper can be obtained. Retirement ends all this social contact.

Some retirees seem not to mind. They may always have felt on edge at work. The incidental contacts of the day may have been annoyances. Their interactions with coworkers may have been competitive rather than supportive, and they may be pleased to be rid of hostile bosses. Or they may simply now be content with the quieter life of retirement. But most retirees seem at first unsettled by the quiet. They feel like a child staying home from school when all the other children of the neighborhood have gone.

The prevalence of social isolation in the days following retirement is hard to determine, because it tends to be underreported. It may exist without being noticed: moderate social isolation can seem like only a temporary absence of things to do, remediable by finding a book to read or a household task or by going for a walk. The realization that life has gone silent can take a while to sink in.

Furthermore, should a retiree become aware of a restlessness associated with being alone, he or she may prefer not to complain about it. The retiree may feel at fault for not adapting more successfully to retirement. And no one wants to be seen as a complainer. Nor does social isolation ordinarily persist more than a few months. Given time and effort, new associations are likely to be developed. Social isolation may then be forgotten.

A few of our respondents, however, reported severe and long-lasting social isolation following their departure from work. Their isolation could neither escape their notice nor be treated as a brief discomfort. One such person was Mrs. Oliver, a former office manager. Mrs. Oliver had gone to work on leaving high school; she said her family had needed her contribution to the family income. She continued to work, mostly in low-level office jobs, until the birth of her first child. She returned to work when her third and last child began school. The job she then found was as a data entry person in a government office. She turned out to be a quick learner and soon was helping coworkers deal with computer problems. Eventually she became the office manager.

Not long after her return to work Mrs. Oliver's husband suffered a back injury in a work accident. He was thereafter considered permanently disabled by his former employer. Actually, his only physical limitation seemed to be that he walked slowly. Most weekdays he would fix his own breakfast—Mrs. Oliver having left for work—and then, around ten, head for a senior center where he read the newspaper and played cards. At noon he would join a friend for lunch, either at the center or at a nearby fast-food restaurant. Except when the weather was bad, he and the friend would follow this with a leisurely walk. By two he would have returned to the senior center. Between four and five he would walk home.

A couple of years before our first interview with Mrs. Oliver, Mr. Oliver put down his cards during one of the morning card games and said he was dizzy and did not feel well. One of the center's staff members drove him to a hospital emergency room, where he was told he had had a heart attack.

Mrs. Oliver almost retired then. She was approaching her mid-sixties and was already eligible for retirement. Her retirement would be practical financially: she and her husband received rent from two apartments, her husband had his disability payments, and Mrs. Oliver would have a pension. She worried that her husband might have another heart attack, but this time one that would be fatal, and she wanted to be with him for whatever time remained to them. On the other hand, she liked her job. She was trying to make up her mind about retirement when her boss, a political appointee, was replaced.

I might have stayed if my boss had stayed. But another half of me was, why not enjoy what my husband and I have together? If it is going to be just for a while, why not enjoy it together? I think I was ready at that point, too.

I had gone back [to work]; I had done my thing; I had achieved something that I never had expected. And once we got to a point where I knew we could be independent and not have to depend on our children, then I knew I could retire.

Mr. Oliver was pleased to have his wife retired and at home, but he continued to leave midmorning for the senior center and he continued to remain there until the late afternoon, just as before his wife's retirement. To her surprise, Mrs. Oliver discovered that the days alone were difficult.

At first it was terrible, lonely. I was used to being out with people. Retirement never meant to me to stay home and do nothing. And it was sad. I'd wake up and I'd say, "Where am I going?" "What am I going to do today?" There was a certain loss at that point. And I think I had to almost go through a grieving period. I used to walk a lot. I would take long walks every day.

Mrs. Oliver imposed structure on the day by listing tasks that needed doing and then setting about them: getting the garden in order; straightening up the house; cleaning.

Fortunately, when I retired, it was summertime. It was in June. So it was a good time for me. I had all the sunshine, the days were long, and I could be out. I had the garden, so I could go out in the yard, work out there. And there were lots of things in the house that I had let go I could start doing again. So I got into cleaning the attic and cleaning the basement and doing lots of things like that, that had just been put on the back burner for years.

I've always found that to keep busy was a salvation for me. It was like as long as you kept busy, you were fine. And when I'd get depressed or get down, I'd walk.

Mrs. Oliver told her husband that she was lonely and wanted him home more. Mr. Oliver said that he understood but he liked having lunch out and he liked spending the afternoon at the senior center. Mrs. Oliver said to us she could respect her husband for knowing what he wanted. But gradually Mrs. Oliver's husband began leaving later in the morning for the senior center, although he continued to meet his friend for lunch.

Mrs. Oliver arranged with a daughter-in-law to look after the daughter-in-law's two young girls, her grandchildren, for part of the afternoon. Mr. Oliver then began coming home earlier so he could be with the grandchildren. Mrs. Oliver, accompanied by her husband, began taking the grandchildren to museums and parks. In only a couple of weeks the Olivers discovered themselves to have become members of a loose community of parents and grandparents caring for young children.

Fortunately, at that time we had our young grandchildren. My daughter-in-law, God bless her, was always good about letting us take the kids and spend time with them. So I guess that helped me get back into a world that wasn't job oriented, meeting other people while we were out and about. At different places we'd meet people that we would never have met if we were just staying home being retired. So we found that by going out with the kids we were affected in our life in a way that we needed.

During her years of work Mrs. Oliver had regularly talked with friends by telephone. Now she arranged to meet the friends for lunch or coffee. One of the friends suggested a cruise they could take with their husbands. Mrs. Oliver liked the idea and began planning for it. Another of the friends suggested that Mrs. Oliver sign up for a crafts course given through the senior center. There were actually two courses being given, one introductory, the other advanced. Mrs. Oliver attended each for a time, then dropped out of the advanced course. Six months after her retirement Mrs. Oliver no longer felt socially isolated.

Some respondents were less successful than Mrs. Oliver in finding a social community that would replace the community their work had provided. One of them, Dr. Sila, a former laboratory scientist, had been absorbed by scientific work throughout her career and, more than most, felt marooned by retirement.

Dr. Sila had none of Mrs. Oliver's nonoccupational links to others when she retired. Before her retirement her social relationships had been almost solely with colleagues. Dr. Sila and her husband were childless, and so Dr. Sila had been without the parent's need to form friendships away from work. Nor had her husband been much help in establishing a network of friends: Dr. Sila's husband, a businessman, was as absorbed in his work as Dr. Sila had been in hers.

In addition, Dr. Sila's dissatisfaction with her ability to express herself in English may have contributed to diffidence when meeting people other than colleagues. Dr. Sila had come to this country from her Asian homeland as a graduate student, and her English remained accented and a bit awkward. Still, it is not unusual for scientists to be relatively uninterested in matters outside their field and to have limited social relationships with nonscientists.

You have a group at work, where you are close, and then you invite them; they invite you. It goes like that. But after not doing a job, you are cut off from those type of people always. It is cut off in one way or another.

My husband said it was okay to retire. We can manage without my earning. If it is your choice, it is okay. My husband said, "You earned your retirement anyways," because I worked for forty years. Forty years is enough; you have done enough.

Unless you get bored. With retirement there is a problem: it is boring some-times. See, if you are in circulation, you know so many things. You are in touch with educated people. You have some exchange of ideas and other things. When you are at home, even great ideas you would have, who would you share with? Sometimes you feel you are cut off from the culture of educated people – cut off, completely cut off.

We talked with Dr. Sila not quite a year after her retirement. By then she had volunteered with a Meals on Wheels program, but she con-tinued to feel isolated. She still missed going to the laboratory. Often, she permitted herself to be housebound:

Sometimes, suppose it is a small storm or something like when weather is not good. You have no purpose to go anywhere. If you are doing the job, you always go somewhere – even in the bad weather. Except [when] it is really tough, you go somewhere, so you are with some people. But when you are retired, and if it is stormy, you have nothing except yourself.

If it is good weather, I can go out. Nine-thirty to twelve, maybe sometimes one-thirty, I go out – shopping, some volunteer work, something. One-thirty, I watch three soap operas. Then four o'clock comes and then tea and a snack. And then the evening meal.

But in the bad weather, if it is raining very hard, you say, why should I go to-day? I don't drive. So most of the time I have to go with the public transport. And when snow is there, the walking footpath they never clean up too much. Once or twice I had a bad experience of falling down on the snow. So you think, really, is it worth going today or not? No. So you put off going. So at that time you feel cut off more.

Not being able to drive may have made it more difficult for Dr. Sila to continue her relationships with her former colleagues. The col-leagues mostly had families and lived in suburbs where public trans-portation became unavailable in the evening. In addition, Dr. Sila's relationships with colleagues had been based on their shared work.

Perhaps it should not be surprising that Dr. Sila was unable to rem-edy her social isolation as had Mrs. Oliver. Dr. Sila had no already es-tablished friendships away from work, and no family in the immediate area. Mrs. Oliver's existing connections made her aware of resources that might have been a bit more difficult for Dr. Sila to locate. Classes at a senior center were as much available to Dr. Sila as they were to Mrs. Oliver, but only Mrs. Oliver found her way to them. Also, Mrs. Oliver may have been more willing to chance new experiences. Dr. Sila's problems with English may have discouraged her from exploring groups like those sponsored by senior centers. And, just possibly, Dr. Sila's desire to maintain her identity as a scientist could have made her unwilling to define herself in another way.

The nature of their marriages may also have played a role in the different experiences of Mrs. Oliver and Dr. Sila. Neither woman's husband made it a priority to help his wife adapt to retirement. Mrs. Oliver's husband was sympathetic to her problems but wanted to maintain his routine; Dr. Sila's husband was preoccupied with his own concerns. But when Mrs. Oliver began establishing a routine that took her out of her home, her husband was available to join her; Dr. Sila's husband would not have been.

Marriage and Social Isolation

As Mrs. Oliver's account may demonstrate, marriage is a resource in the management of social isolation. As both her account and the account of Dr. Sila illustrate, marriage is not in itself a remedy for social isolation.

The ways in which marriage can be helpful may be evident in an account provided by a former lawyer, Mr. Foster. Mr. Foster's experience of social isolation had come about in his mid-forties, when he left his position with an established law firm. He thereafter did legal work occasionally but more often worked as a carpenter. The two occupations together only rarely provided forty hours of work per week and with some frequency provided no work at all. By the time Mr. Foster declared himself retired, he had already been underemployed for about twenty years. Indeed, he was pleased to have reached his mid-sixties because now he could declare himself retired.

One of the problems I had was that I sort of held myself out to the world as a practicing lawyer, whereas in fact I did not have a sufficiently active practice to really earn a living. And I didn't like the false pretenses of all that. So when I reached the magic number of sixty-five, I could quite gladly say, okay now, I'm retired. And that took care of the problem of living under a false impression.

Whenever somebody asks me, "What are you doing?" I say, "Well, I'm retired." I told people that I wasn't taking on any new business; I might handle a small matter now and then for somebody I've known for a long time, but that's about the size of it.

Mr. Foster had been asked to leave his firm while still in his forties after he failed to respond to senior partners' warnings. They had received complaints from clients of woozy interchanges with him and had made their own observations of his afternoon naps. The partner who carried the message acknowledged that Mr. Foster did well in court, but said that he was an alcoholic and should get help. His office smelled like a brewery, the partner said, and the firm could not tolerate it any longer.

After his dismissal Mr. Foster set up practice in his home. But he continued to drink, and the practice did not amount to much. There were confrontations with his wife and threats of divorce. He then joined Alcoholics Anonymous. After a couple of months he left Alcoholics Anonymous because he felt that it was too preachy and joined a hospital-based support group for recovering alcoholics. That worked. When we talked with him, he had been sober for more than twenty years.

With Mr. Foster's sobriety established, the Fosters' lives settled down. But they discovered that their friends had dropped away. There was no one they felt entirely comfortable calling. Mr. Foster, in talking with us, said that the former friends had either moved to other parts of the country or had become busy with their families.

Mr. Foster's wife had continued to work and so was largely protected from social isolation, but Mr. Foster was not so fortunate. He was on friendly terms with neighbors, with whom he would now and again chat, but otherwise he appeared on his way to becoming a recluse. Perhaps for his sake as well as her own, Mrs. Foster decided to become more active in her neighborhood community. She began attending a nearby church and found the congregation accepting and the minister friendly. She cajoled Mr. Foster into accompanying her to

Sunday services. Soon Mr. Foster became more involved in the life of the church. He provided legal advice to its committees. He helped set up an accounting system. He replaced rotted boards on a porch. He joined the choir. When he talked with us, he had become an influential member of the congregation.

It seemed that a lot of our friends had moved away and whatever, and my wife was feeling a lack of friends, and so she started going to the church. I didn't go but she told me, "I think you'll like the minister and I think you'll like the choir, and why don't you come along?" So I did. And I liked both. And then I found myself quickly drawn into a lot of church activities, particularly in the legal and financial end of things and the choir. And I have been kind of a jack-of-all-trades around the church, anything, helping work on the building, everything.

I would say I'm part of the leadership of the church just because I've been around the church for twenty years or so, because the church congregation can change a lot as people move. People don't stay put in this country. So just as the person who's been involved in the center of church activities for over twenty years, I would say I'm part of the church leadership.

Last night I went to a meeting with the minister and a couple of other people. A project that this one fellow is working on, he asked me to attend the meeting because I handle a lot of the financial stuff and it was a question of how it is going to be financed. And he felt that he wants to go to the governing board of the church, and he feels that if I recommend his project it would help to carry weight.

On days when Mr. Foster had nothing to do at the church, he kept the house in order, gardened, and busied himself with projects: for instance, he spent a day upholstering a chair. Asked about his social life, Mr. Foster spoke of sisters and brothers who lived at a distance, his grown children, his neighbors, and his church associations. But he still felt isolated socially. The church membership was important but did not help him feel accepted within the community of people with whom he had gone to law school and people with whom he had worked. He felt a bit like someone who had been exiled from the place in which he really belonged. When we asked him what problems he was encountering in retirement, he said:

Probably the biggest problem is the community. That goes back to my failure vocationally. And for a man, particularly, what he does vocationally is so much tied up with his self-concept and self-esteem.

I tend to get depressed easily, particularly if I am alone. When I'm with people I'm not depressed. As a matter of fact, I think most people I know say I'm sort of a humorous guy. And I get along well with people. But I'm alone too much. It's a problem for me.

I'd be much happier if I could look back and see a vocationally successful life. I'd feel a much stronger sense of belonging to the whole community if I had that.

Mr. Foster's marriage helped him establish membership in one community but could not help with the community he felt he had reluctantly left years ago. Nor could it substitute for membership in that community.

Mr. Foster's wife was an active participant in her own community of work. But Mr. Foster could gain no sense of vicarious membership in that community by listening to his wife's discussion of its events; on the contrary, his wife's talking about what happened in her office made Mr. Foster feel worse. It underscored the barrenness of his own life.

When she's talking about sort of office politics, if so and so is mad at so and so, that has a bearing on her own life but it isn't all that interesting to me. I make an effort to be interested, because I think she needs somebody she can talk to when she comes home. And I feel that I should listen to her because if I don't she would be unhappy and it would be bad for our marriage. If I do that, it just helps things go better between us, and it's reflected in how she acts towards me, her conversation and everything else. But sometimes I feel that she is so wrapped up in her work and what she has to do here at home that she doesn't pay enough attention to what I might be feeling.

A retiree's marriage can help him or her deal with social isolation, but it will not end the isolation. It can even, as happened occasionally with Mr. Foster, make it more painful.[1] What is needed to end social isolation is a network of others among whom one is known and valued: a community in which one has a place. During the career years, that can be provided by work. In retirement, membership in other communities must be sought.

The Nature of Social Isolation

Social isolation is a distressing emotional state that results specifically from the absence of membership in a community of emotional importance. It is different from the loneliness to which people are vulnerable when there is no one with whom to partner their emotional lives.[2] It can be experienced as a world gone quiet, as having been exiled from the active social world, as not being wanted. It implies having no one to visit and no social events to take part in. Without membership in a social network, there are no invitations to outings, no gatherings or parties. There is no need to leave the house except to shop for necessities or to walk the dog.

Social isolation is not depression. There is no persisting loss of faith in the self, as happens in depression. And while depression is resistive to being dispelled, the discomfort of social isolation disappears when the people who were isolated become engaged in social activity. Nor is isolation produced by the way people feel about themselves, as often is depression. It comes about for other reasons—such as retirement—although once established it can then affect the way people feel about themselves.[3]

Very occasionally people recognize that they are isolated and insist that being isolated is just fine. Interaction with others makes them anxious or angry, and they would just as soon not have it. But even for them, social isolation has severe costs. They are without the friends or acquaintances with whom favors can be exchanged. They lack access to the information and advice others might provide about important issues like who is a good doctor and less important issues like what is worth seeing at the movies. They have no conversational partner who will listen to them as they think through plans and who will respond with criticism or useful support. Boredom occurs almost solely within a context of social isolation. If there are active associations with others, there are things to do.

Research suggests that social isolation increases vulnerability to physical illness and, among those already ill, brings death closer.[4] Mr. Foster's participation in the life of his church almost surely was beneficial to his health. James House offers this summary of what has been found:

Social isolation has been shown repeatedly to prospectively predict mortality and serious morbidity both in general population samples and in individuals with established morbidity, especially coronary heart disease. The magnitude of risk associated with social isolation is comparable with that of cigarette smoking and other major biomedical and psychosocial risk factors.[5]

Most retirees develop fully adequate relational lives. Many develop a mix of relationships that includes friends, family, neighbors, and people met in the course of their retirement activities. Family may become more important than it had been, as may membership in a voluntary organization. Some retirees add voluntary activities to an already full social life centered on friends and family: they might participate in a church, participate in a book club, give time to a charity, and take part in community politics. Some retirees become active in their neighborhoods, making a point to talk to neighbors, doing favors, and supervising the neighborhood children.

Kin ties by themselves, without other relationships, do not seem to work for most respondents as a basis for feeling integrated into the larger society. The concerns of kin to keep up with one another's lives and to help each other should need arise are too insular to link people to the concerns of the larger society. Nor do kin relationships support identities other than being someone's parent or sibling or child. In addition, kin are often spread out geographically, so that visiting is with one member of the family or another, but not with the family together. Yet respondents were often pleased if they lived near a family member with whom they could share holiday celebrations as well as occasional meals through the year, exchange favors, and talk—sometimes almost daily—about the news of their lives.

The level of sociability that retirees established seemed to be a continuation of the level of nonwork sociability they had maintained before their retirements. A very wide range of sociability seemed satisfactory. Some retirees maintained a very active social life: in one instance, a retiree belonged to boards of community organizations, participated in local political organizations, and kept up with a good many friends. Other retirees found equal satisfaction in much quieter lives, in which they kept in touch with family and a small number of friends, and spent most evenings at home.

The retired who were without life partners were likely to have special problems with retirement. Because of the absence of anyone who shared their emotional lives, they were vulnerable to loneliness. The loneliness was unlikely to be constant, however. More likely, they would find themselves suddenly lonely at times when people might expect to be accompanied by someone emotionally close: in the early evening, perhaps on the weekend, at weddings.

During the working years people on their own could manage loneliness more easily because of having work. Weekends might be dreary, but the workweek would be filled with social events: sharing work on projects, participating in meetings, joining others for lunch. Retirement cost them work's distractions and supports.

Besides making for greater vulnerability to the distress of loneliness, retirement brought with it new vulnerability to social isolation. Retirees who were on their own had more trouble than others in establishing membership in new communities: they had no partner to help them locate possible activities and to bolster their courage when they thought about investigating them.

One never-married retiree was Ms. Putnam, the former college administrator whose job was important enough to her that she arranged to come in for a few weekends after her formal retirement to finish a project. Interviewed two years after her retirement, Ms. Putnam described an active social life with a wide circle of acquaintances. She had lunch with former coworkers once or twice a month. She would occasionally bump into an acquaintance while shopping and might then stop for coffee and conversation. Twice during the two years since retirement she had traveled in Europe with a friend. She was active as a volunteer for the college she had attended, helping in its alumni office with reunions and serving on a search committee. She helped edit a newsletter produced by a neighborhood group. Yet these sporadic contacts were unrelated to one another. They did not together constitute a continuing community.

Ms. Putnam also maintained relationships within a large family. Here there was indeed a network, as there was not among her friends and acquaintances. Ms. Putnam was a good great-aunt to the children of her nephews and nieces. One afternoon a week she took one or the other of her two grandnieces for an outing. One of the grandnieces would occasionally sleep over in her apartment. Once or twice a year Ms. Putnam visited family who lived at a distance, usually to attend a wedding or a funeral. Her contacts with kin provided Ms. Putnam with a sense of membership in a network of mutual concern. Yet they did not connect her to the wider world. In her kin relationships Ms. Putnam was an aunt and a great-aunt, nothing more.

Ms. Putnam was determinedly cheerful. She had said, before her retirement, that she was looking forward to leaving her job. A year after her retirement Ms. Putnam said that although her life had changed radically, she was as busy as she wanted to be. Yet the interviewer felt unconvinced by her cheerfulness. When the interviewer asked Ms. Putnam whether she missed any part of her work, she responded, "I miss people," and the interviewer thought there was special emotional force in this comment.

In retirement, Ms. Putnam had neither the distractions nor the reassurances of work. Her days might contain one or two social events but were mostly spent alone. Her evenings were more often alone than not. The interviewer asked Ms. Putnam whether she was sometimes lonely and Ms. Putnam said yes, she could feel lonely, but there were always people to call. Loneliness, she suggested, was easily manageable.

If you feel lonely, there are so many people who would be so happy to have a telephone call. I know that I can pick up the phone and talk to any number of people. There's a woman who's retired and is living in a retirement complex that I worked with for many years, and she is now legally blind, and every so often I will call her and talk for a half hour or so. And I have some friends who are all in their late seventies into their late eighties and I will call and talk with them.

And we have some neighbors, former neighbors, who lived across the street from us when we were growing up, and they are going to be married sixty years the end of June, and their family is having a little celebration for them. And I pick up the phone every so often and call them.

In truth, having so many people to call did little to diminish Ms. Putnam's loneliness. There was no one among the recipients of her calls with whom Ms. Putnam's life was shared, to whom she could even say, "I feel lonely."

After completing the interview from which the preceding excerpt was taken, our interviewer wrote, "Whenever we got into the area of being alone . . . the respondent would tear up; her face would crumple. I thought she was going to cry and at a couple of points at the end of the interview she wiped tears from her eyes. She did all this even while protesting that she never felt alone, liked being by herself, and always had things to do."

There is much to admire in Ms. Putnam's minimization of what appears to be both occasional loneliness and moderate social isolation. She was doing the best she could with an unpromising situation, and part of her approach was to look on its brighter aspects. Another respondent, Mrs. Chalmers, in a situation similar to Ms. Putnam's, simply accepted her doubly isolated state and allowed herself to become something of a recluse.

Mrs. Chalmers was divorced, with two grown daughters, one living near her, the other in a distant city. Mrs. Chalmers had been an executive in a publishing house, but as she neared retirement age she began experiencing symptoms she ascribed to stress: sleeplessness, sudden inexplicable tearfulness. She took a leave from her work. After a year on leave she retired.

We first talked with Mrs. Chalmers about a month after her retirement. At that time she thought she might travel. She would have to go alone, but in the past she had rather liked traveling alone. So far, though, she had not been able to organize herself enough to decide on a destination.

We saw Mrs. Chalmers again a year later. She had not traveled anywhere. Indeed, she had not done much of anything. She had taken no classes, joined no groups, seen almost no friends. She had gotten together with the daughter who lived not far from her two or three times a week, and they had attended concerts and movies together. Her primary companions were her two dachshunds. She intended to be more active in the year to follow.

We saw Mrs. Chalmers yet again two years after her retirement. Her life had not changed at all. We asked, in this interview, how she spent her days. She said:

I usually go to bed very late, so I wake up late. I let my dogs out the back yard, put up the coffee, take in the newspaper, scan page one and the editorial page, get dressed, take my dogs for a walk. And the rest of the day, I sit on the couch. In the morning, or what is left of the morning, there's nothing on television, so I read. And that ranges widely from books to magazines to the newspapers. Yesterday I was reading a couple of Wall Street Journals that my daughter brought over. And then I got two new mystery magazines; I was reading those. And then in the afternoon there are two game shows on TV, so I watch those.

And then I walk the dogs again, like early evening. And then I either watch television or, when that's done, that's the time I turn on some of my records, my tapes, listen to some marvelous music. If there's something on television at night, I will watch it. I usually watch news at eleven.

This is a startlingly isolated life. Mrs. Chalmers spent many of her days without contact with anyone other than her daughter.

If I didn't have the dogs, I'd probably never go out of the house except to shop for food, and that could be a shopping for one day for the week. I resent having to walk the dogs in the snow, or when it gets very, very, windy, yet I know that they're my link with the world.

Mrs. Chalmers believed that her isolation, which she fully recognized, was a consequence of her retirement. She had always been a bit tense when with people she did not know well. Now that she had retired, she was no longer required to subject herself to the anxieties of interaction.

I think it's retirement—living alone, without any need to be out in the world. In retirement you have that opportunity to not be out in the world. A lot of things probably subconsciously surface. My basic insecurities. My feeling that there's a lot less pressure when you're not with people in terms of doing well with people, being liked by people. All these things that kids go through that you stop thinking about when you have a job and you have to get it done and you work with people and you get along fine with them. It wasn't that I hated being a part of the social world. I loved it. But I also, equally, like not having to be tested.

I thought that after a year of this hibernation I would be ready to go and to make friends again and to think again. I thought after a year I'd go back. And it's been lots more than that and I haven't.

Mrs. Chalmers was, of course, lonely. Like Ms. Putnam, she teared up when reviewing her situation, although for her the interview was a welcome interruption of her isolation. But she insisted that she had become adapted to being alone. Indeed, her social isolation had become self-sustaining. If she were to call someone, what could she say she had been doing? How could she explain calling out of the blue?

It becomes more difficult to pick up the phone, for example, to maybe call an old friend, because they're going to say, "What've you been doing?" And I find it difficult to say, "Nothing." Which is the actual truth. Not that they won't think well of me, but that I wouldn't. I feel disappointed in myself.

Other respondents retired not long after having been widowed. They too had a hard time of it.

Mr. Martin, an accountant, lost his much loved wife to cancer two years before the date when they had long intended to retire together. Their full plan was to buy a home in Europe and to live part of the year there, part of the year in this country. With his wife's death Mr. Martin lost his belief that there could be anything good in his future and all ability to plan for it.

Our first interview with Mr. Martin took place about a year after his wife's death. Mr. Martin was having severe difficulties in meeting his obligations to his clients. His grief interfered with his ability to do his work.

I'm not coping very well. I've sort of retreated. I think after my wife's death I was in shock. This year it seems to have hit me. I miss her. And as far as my practice is concerned, I really have to push myself. Absolutely have to push myself. I keep procrastinating. For instance, what I've got to do today is get out tax extensions on about fifty percent of the returns I'm responsible for. I keep putting them aside and putting them aside until I get to the point of no return.

I date it from two years before my wife's death. I started slowly going to pieces when it became obvious my wife was terminally ill. And I haven't put the pieces together yet. I got very disorganized. I wasn't keeping up my accounts. I kept forgetting things.

I write notes to myself. Memos stare me in the face, I still forget. I keep telling myself that I've got to get out of this before someone hits me with a suit.

We talked with Mr. Martin two years later. He had by then retired. He continued to do tax work for a few clients of long standing but referred new business to his former firm. The death of his wife had ended his link to what had been his network of friends. Loss of that network, plus retirement, made for nearly complete social isolation.

My wife and I were in this group of professionals, a very close-knit group. And almost every two weeks someone in the group would give a party. I no longer socialize with this group, unless one of the people happens to invite me. They're friendly enough when I show up. But I know definitely some of them don't invite me. A couple of times I've been told they haven't been able to reach me: "We called your house and couldn't get you" and so forth.

Mr. Martin had been asked to help organize a reunion of his college class. His spirits were raised by being involved in organizing the class's fortieth reunion. He felt that he had returned to his old self during the two weeks of preparation for the reunion and the three days of the reunion itself, with its meetings, seminars, and parties.

The last couple of weeks I've been on a pretty even keel because I got involved in reunion activities. I was on one committee and I had to present a paper at a seminar. I think the high point was a sort of mini-reunion with people I'd gone to high school with. That was very nice. We were all very close—a very close-knit, a competitive yet friendly, group. It was nice seeing them. I saw some people I hadn't seen for fifty years. The reunion was a lot of fun. I thoroughly enjoyed it.

Our interview took place a week after the reunion. By then the glow from the reunion was fading. Mr. Martin's one positive thought was that if he could find another marriage partner, he might be able to reestablish his life. But he was in his mid-sixties, and felt awkward once again to be dating.

One of my friends said at the reunion last week, "When you find yourself a woman, all this will disappear." I think there's a lot of truth in that. But finding a woman is hard. I don't find it easy to call women for dates. Picking up the phone—for me I'm back in my teenage years. Basically it's a fear of rejection.

Because Mr. Martin had no partner to help him sustain his belief in himself, he was made anxious by the risk of reaching out to others. He had made some efforts but they had not worked out, and he was reluctant to try again.

Perhaps Mr. Martin should not have retired, although he had lost his appetite for work and his work had been going badly. He might have done better to have cut his workload by around two-thirds, down to an easy two days, by retaining the clients who had been with him longest and referring his other clients to his former firm. The absence of all connection with his former community of work, when added to the loss of his life partner, was more than he could manage.

Another respondent, Mr. Evans, was initially in a situation like that of Mr. Martin, but did remarry. Mr. Evans had been widowed some three years before we first talked with him. He was then a year away from a scheduled retirement.

Mr. Evans had four children, three of them married, one, a son, newly divorced. The son suggested to Mr. Evans that they share an apartment. Although Mr. Evans was very lonely, he declined the offer. He wanted to reestablish his own life, which for him meant to remarry, and he thought living with his son would constitute a detour.

We returned to talk with Mr. Evans not long after his retirement. We learned that for several months he had been attending dances for unmarried seniors and at one of the dances had met someone he hoped to marry. He said he needed someone to talk with and travel with. He was much less lonely.

A year later Mr. Evans had remarried. His new wife planned to retire soon herself. The two had an active and satisfying social life. Mr. Evans was delighted with once again having a partner in life and being a member of a social community. He had almost forgotten how lonely he had been.

We go out on the weekends. And we have a group of friends that are in our own age group that we will go to dances or things like that with, that the Knights of Columbus run, or whatever. Or we'll just have a house party. And on Sunday mornings or Saturdays we might go out for breakfast or brunch and meet another couple. And things like this.

Mr. Evans had focused his energies on finding a life partner and a sustaining community. He found what might be called a transitional community first: the dances for single seniors. He then met someone with whom he could form the partnership he wanted. With her help he regained membership in a social community that provided the support and social engagement he needed.

Mr. Evans seemed not to have been hurt by his retirement. On the contrary, his retirement seems to have given him a freedom from obligation that facilitated his efforts to repair his social world. Perhaps he was able to use that freedom because enough time had passed since his bereavement. Perhaps he was unusually determined to make his life better.

Chapter Six

Using the Time of Retirement

Whatever retirees choose to do in the time they once gave to work, the activities should, ideally, sustain their feelings of worth, be intellectually and emotionally rewarding, and reduce their vulnerability to social isolation. Furthermore, the activities should not be overly demanding: the obligations they entail should be limited and virtually stress free. Otherwise, as retirees sometimes remark, why retire? All this is quite a lot to ask of any particular retirement activity, but it is entirely possible to put together a mix of activities that together fill the bill.[1]

This chapter considers the contributions likely to be made by each of the major categories of retirement activities: part-time work; volunteering; participation in organized programs; hobbies, games, and sports; travel; and puttering. As David Ekerdt has pointed out, our society tends to respect most highly those who have a productive, even strenuous, retirement: who develop post-retirement businesses or become serious musicians or artists or take adventuresome trips.[2] A few of our respondents gave credence to this "busy ethic" by initially exaggerating how much time they spent doing things and understating how much they spent reading the newspaper or watching television or visiting a mall or puttering. That said, it should be noted that many of our respondents kept very full schedules and none engaged in unsatisfying activities just to appear active.

In the following discussion of the contributions of the activities engaged in by retirees I do not distinguish between the activities' possibly different value for men and for women. But in our sample sometimes there did seem to be subtle difference between men and women in the kinds of postretirement activities they found attractive.

Men in our sample seemed to respond more to activities in which they could display competence or effectiveness. They seemed somewhat more likely than the women in the sample to take on administrative roles in voluntary associations. Some found competitive activities such as golf to be absorbing. Women, on the other hand, seemed more likely to seek opportunities to be with congenial people and more likely to find attractive the role of helper. Also, more than men, they seemed to want retirement associations in which mutual concern was manifest.[3]

These differences between men and women should not be exaggerated. Some women were attracted to competitive activities like bridge; some men sought opportunities to function as helpers with, for example, Meals on Wheels. In this chapter I describe Mrs. Oliver's pleasure in her competence as a seamstress and Mr. Abbott's pleasure in helping others.

Part-Time Work as a Retirement Activity

One activity high on retirees' list of attractive things to do with their new free time is work. But in the context of retirement, retirees did not view work as they had during their careers, when work was the major determinant of where and how they lived, when they were able to pay their bills, and who they were; rather, they viewed work as an attractive way of using some of their leisure time.

Retirement work should be distinguished from the work that may be preliminary to retirement. In the latter, people ease into retirement by cutting back on hours or relinquishing their most demanding tasks.[4] Jobs that are transitional to retirement, as when the owner of a family firm reduces his responsibilities by giving some of them to a son, or when an academic goes on half-time while continuing to teach essential courses, might be called "bridge jobs." Whether a particular job is a bridge job rather than retirement work would depend on

whether the job is a station on the way to full retirement or a gratifying use of the time made available by a retirement that has already
occurred.[5]

The gratification of work in retirement can take many forms. Like
the work that was done during the retiree's career, it can structure the
week by providing somewhere to go, a time to be there, and, once
there, responsibilities. It can keep the retiree in touch with others in
an occupational community. If the retirement work requires professional skills or acting in a professional role, it can help maintain the
retiree's identity as a professional. It can reassure the retiree that he or
she remains capable of occupational contribution.[6]

One respondent, Mrs. Rogers, had had a successful career in a large
firm, beginning as a secretary and ending as an office manager. On retiring, Mrs. Rogers discovered that her employment record was two
quarters short of qualification for Social Security. To make up those
quarters, she took a job as a full-time secretary in a bank.

I turned sixty-five and I wasn't planning to work. Then I discovered that I didn't
have enough quarters. So I had to work to get the quarters. That's when I went
and joined the bank. I started five days because I wanted to make the quarters as fast as I could.

Once Mrs. Rogers met Social Security requirements, she stopped
working full time. But she did want work as a retirement activity. She
had never married, and her friendships were limited. She wanted the
social contact that work provided.

Mrs. Rogers experimented a bit with how much work would give
her the best combination of engagement and freedom. After trying
three days a week, she decided two days would be optimal.

I just worked the five days because I had to. At this stage of the game I didn't
really want to. I've got too many other things I like to do. So I cut back to three
days. And then last year a bunch of holidays all came on a Monday, so I had
these Mondays off. And it was such a lovely feeling that I decided I'd never
work on Monday again. Most people hate getting up Monday morning. It's
different on Tuesday. You don't mind getting up on Tuesday. So I cut back to
two days.

Mrs. Rogers wanted part-time work to avoid social isolation. Living alone, and with a diminished social circle, she was especially vulnerable to social isolation and especially likely to need a community provided by work. In addition, working reassured her that she remained someone of value in the world of work.

I don't have very many friends. They've either died or moved away. And so it's better to be with people. And anyway, I really just like being useful. If you're not working, you feel sort of useless.

Like Mrs. Rogers, other respondents reported that they felt that two days a week, plus or minus a few hours, was about the right amount of time to give to retirement work. That was enough to fend off feelings of marginality but not so much that their free time was unduly invaded. It also helped if the time they had to work was flexible, as it apparently was for Mrs. Rogers.

Mr. Marquis, the former businessman who retired from his business career after a heart attack, had searched unsuccessfully for a hobby in retirement. After a year of restlessness, he became a customer service representative for the firm that during his career had been his major competitor.

I went and got hold of what used to be my biggest competitor. We've known each other for years and had admiration for each other, even though we were competitors. And I said to him, "Phil, how about a job? I just want a place to put my hat." And he said, "Sure, couldn't think of a nicer guy. Come on." So I came in as a member of the customer relations group. The regime that I've been working on is nine to one, five days a week. And I have plenty of things to do, good and important things. Customer service. It's small, but it makes me feel that I'm not a charity case.

So I'm back working again, because I love working. I think my hobby, my pleasure, and my total enjoyment outside of my family is working. I find that in working I'm in constant contact with other people. I love people. I enjoy them. I think people keep you alert, sharp, and going. And I feel I'm that much younger for my contact of being with people. There is such a thing as having, like they say, a place to hang your hat. And I have a place to hang my hat every day.

In keeping with the job being a retirement activity, Mr. Marquis was able to take time off as he wanted to. The job did not prevent him from realizing, to a satisfactory degree, retirement's freedom from constraint.

They treat me in a very respectful manner. In the beginning I told them, "I'll be late this morning" or "I have to go home early" or "I got a doctor's appointment this afternoon." "Don't ever tell us that again. Don't be ridiculous. You come and go. You want vacation, don't ask. Just let us know when you're going."

Mr. Marquis's job was useful, engaging, and virtually stress free. It permitted Mr. Marquis to take time off when he wanted to. It could hardly have been bettered as retirement work.

Professionals and academics seemed to find it somewhat easier than former executives and administrators to continue the parts of their work that had been gratifying during their careers while jettisoning the parts that had been stressful or unpleasant. Professor Blair, a former professor of humanities, retired when he was sixty-eight. He had planned to retire a couple of years later than he did, but when his wife became ill, and at the same time his dean refused to approve his department's hiring of a junior faculty person he was sponsoring, he decided to advance the retirement date. After his retirement he liked telling people that he had taken early retirement, since he retired before reaching seventy.

Professor Blair arranged with a neighboring university's extension service to teach a single course during one semester each year. It was important to him that he was able to continue to teach. He was pleased that he no longer suffered the stresses of faculty life.

I am retired, and I'm now seeing things from a distance. And I want it that way. That's what old age is all about, I think, to be able to see reality dispassionately. As long as you are part of the crew of a ship, you fight for your own life and for everybody else's life because a ship can sink. Now there is a way of watching the ship from outside, from the shore. Let's put it that way. It's a good metaphor.

I'm not only on the shore. I occasionally do step on the ship. I teach extension courses. But that is limited work. It goes almost by inertia. I don't go to faculty meetings. I don't vote; I don't try to influence another colleague in order to have a majority of voting; I don't discuss with another colleague who tries to have my vote, that kind of thing.

The time does come when, not being in politics, one sees better the reality of what politics is about. One sees it better if one is not involved—like watching a ship from the shore.

Dr. Brevis, a retired psychiatrist, continued to see a few patients at home, mostly because he wanted to keep his hand in, although he was also a bit worried about his financial situation and liked continuing to earn income. He limited his practice to patients who would not require a great deal from him. He too found that the right amount of retirement work was two days, plus or minus a few hours. He gave just one day a week to seeing patients, but if occasional attendance at conferences and fairly regular attention to professional journals were added in, he gave his work somewhat more.

I am retired except for one day a week. On Thursdays I see private patients. I don't have a huge patient load, but I have some patients that I have been seeing for a long time. I don't see them all every week, of course. Some I see every month or six weeks even. Some are medication patients and some just need to come in and get a booster from time to time. I don't see anybody more often than every two weeks. I don't know whether I would have more difficulty separating from them or they from me. I think they from me—I would like to terminate with many of them.

I've taken only two new patients since I retired. I'm not asking for referrals because I don't have any hospital affiliations at this point. I don't want any. If I had to hospitalize a patient, I would have to see him or her every day and that wouldn't be retired. So if any of my patients now would have to be hospitalized, I would refer them to someone else. And I wouldn't take on anybody at this point that I felt would need hospitalization. If I'm going to be retired, I want to be retired—except for this one day when I see patients in psychotherapy or medication follow-up.

The additional income that comes with retirement work can be of emotional as well as practical value. It can help meet expenses that retirees may not have anticipated. One of Dr. Brevis's sons had returned to professional school, and Dr. Brevis was helping him with tuition. Dr. Brevis thought of the fees he received from his patients as offsetting the contribution he made to his son's school expenses.

Some other respondents also thought of income from retirement work as offsetting specific costs. Mr. Mitchell, the former warehousing supervisor, took a part-time job as a driver of a delivery truck because his retirement income did not cover the expenses of his photography hobby; driving the truck made the hobby possible.

Some respondents who had no special use for the income they received from retirement work nevertheless spoke of it as making them more comfortable with their financial situation. But quite apart from its potential practical value, being paid mattered because it demonstrated that the work was serious and valuable. Dr. Brevis was like many other professionals in that he would have continued his retirement work even if he had not had a use for the money. His understanding of himself was that he was a psychiatrist, and seeing patients helped him to maintain this identity.

Among professionals, maintaining a professional identity may have been especially important to physicians. All five of the physicians in our sample kept up their licenses despite having formally retired. Four of them continued to practice part time after their retirement: Dr. Brevis saw a few patients in a home office; another, who also saw a few patients in his home, in addition provided physical examinations for a military recruiting office; a third worked half time as the physician in a college health clinic (with summers and intersessions off); and the fourth was titular head of a project in preventive medicine that received day-to-day direction from someone else.

Common to these arrangements was that, everything considered, they required a few hours less than twenty hours a week. In two cases hours were entirely flexible and in the other two they permitted some flexibility. Common also was that the work was virtually stress free; the three retired physicians who saw patients could refer those with serious problems to other doctors.

The retired physician who did not do part-time medical work had health problems of his own that depleted his energy. Nevertheless, he attended talks on medical topics given in a hospital near his home. And when we saw him a year after his retirement, he was contemplating, although only half seriously, a search for a medical post that would be easy and fun; he was wondering about signing on as a cruise ship physician.

None of this is to say there are not retired physicians who have packed away their stethoscopes and devoted their retirement to golf or travel or art. It may be that we missed them by not recruiting respondents from retirement villages and golf course communities. But for those retired physicians for whom medicine had sustained a valued identity, a satisfactory retirement would seem to require continued, if limited, activity as a physician.

The lawyers among our respondents seemed only slightly less interested in maintaining their professional identities. Of our eight former lawyers, three continued to do work for longtime clients; a fourth provided legal assistance to his church; a fifth was actively lobbying a judge he knew for court-related work he could do on his own schedule. The others, it seemed, retained a sense of themselves as former lawyers, although they no longer practiced at all.

Some of the former academics in our sample taught part time. Professor Blair chose to teach evenings; another led tours to archaeological digs; another, a leader in his field, frequently lectured at universities in distant cities; a fourth, a former science professor, agreed to a retirement position in his department in which he became responsible for the allocation of scarce supplies. Another former science professor, although he did little else in his field, regularly attended colloquia, just to keep up.

Among other professionals, a former minister was able to fill in for absent ministers at churches other than the one he had led, and a former scientist was hired back by his firm as a part-time consultant.

Although most retired professionals and academics found part-time work in their fields, most respondents who had been in other careers did not. Much depended on whether the occupation required full-time organizational membership: for example, it is not possible, ordinarily, to be a part-time department head. Administrators, managers, businessmen, engineers, and technicians who had had careers dependent on full-time organizational membership usually did not find opportunity in their fields for part-time contribution. Exceptional were a few retired executives with technical skills, who were able to work part time as consultants to their former firms or to other firms in their fields.

In contrast to the many respondents for whom part-time work was an important part of retirement, other respondents said they had little interest in retirement work. They felt no need to sustain an occupational identity or to maintain even marginal membership within their former work communities. Several respondents had retired in part to escape tasks with which they were bored or which they had come to dislike. Mr. Paige, the former computer engineer, said he was delighted that he would never again have to do the painstaking work required to locate bugs in computer programs.

Some respondents turned down part-time work because they felt that it would be stressful or time-consuming. Mr. Mathers, the former sales manager, turned down an offer to consult for his former firm because he was sure he would become involved in stressful negotiations with customers. Mrs. Alvarez, the former head bookkeeper, discouraged the possibility of part-time work with her former firm partly because she wanted to be home with her husband and partly because she had long resented being undervalued by the firm.

By and large it did not seem as if a sense of diminished skills inhibited respondents from taking on retirement work. Two former academics gave up on plans to write a textbook when they realized they had become too distant from their former fields, but that was more a matter of diminished motivation than a sense of diminished capability.

In general, attitudes toward retirement work varied dramatically. For some of our respondents, it made the difference between a retirement with which they were content and one in which they were constantly restless or bored or threatened by social isolation. For others, it was unattractive to the point of being abhorrent. Perhaps no other way of using the time of retirement was assessed so differently by different respondents.

Volunteering

Retirees who liked serving as volunteers earlier in their lives tended to like volunteering after their retirement. On the other hand, retirees who had not been volunteers before their retirement tended not to be volun-

teers thereafter.[7] One investigator put the matter this way: "A significant number of elderly volunteers may be volunteers who became elderly."[8] If people have not found value in volunteer effort before they
retire, it seems unlikely that they will find value in such effort afterward.

Voluntary activities vary enormously in their demands. Some require so little in skill or training or so little thought that they would
have been rejected as mindless or too close to drudgery had they
been offered as part-time jobs. Examples are driving elderly or infirm parishioners to church, helping at a soup kitchen or delivering
Meals on Wheels. But such voluntary activities are not understood as
low-level jobs by those who commit themselves to performing them.
Rather, they are ways of helping. In spirit they are close to shopping
for an ill neighbor or giving a friend a lift to the airport.

Other voluntary activities may require something approaching a
professional level of skill and knowledge. An example is teaching a
course in photography for an adult education course. And some voluntary activities require assumption of a level of responsibility that
would be appropriate for paid work: for example, acting as treasurer
for a fraternal society. Here, too, the tasks are performed in the spirit
of doing a favor, although a fairly large one.

Doing good may be the one consistent element in the very wide
range of voluntary activities. Voluntary activities help retirees to feel
capable and, more than that, to feel that their efforts benefit others.
Often it matters that the good they do is for an organization or group
with which they can identify. One respondent served as an auxiliary
instructor for a shop class in a high school he had once attended. Another helped in the registrar's office of a small college that her daughter attended.

A couple, the Canfields, were active in a fairly small organization
whose aim was to publicize the need for research on a disease from
which Mrs. Canfield suffered. The organization also attempted to
raise funds for the research. The Canfields had joined the organization
before Mr. Canfield's retirement. After his retirement they decided to
become more active. Mr. Canfield said:

The president was doing it all in her house, and we discussed it and we both
agreed that this lady, the president, needed help. And her husband got very

sick, so that sort of brought it to a head. So it was more or less, "There's a need there; let's do it."

We're fairly healthy people, even though we've had our setbacks. We had to convince the president that our offer was real, but we just started taking over the mailing and then we gradually went into the printing – and whatever else, whatever it takes.

Work for the organization kept the Canfields busy, at times busier than they might have wanted:

Taking over the association mailings and printings and everything else is more than what I thought it was going to be. This past week we've been working on a mailing and working on our picnic. We're having a fund-raiser picnic, and my wife's been making up some baskets to raffle off.

I'm not sure whether it's just because I'm getting older that I'm slowing down or what. But it seems as though it's not enough time in the day to do what we want to do now.

The interviewer asked Mr. Canfield what motivated him to work so hard for the organization. His answer: it gave him an opportunity to do something for others.

It's rewarding. You're doing something to help youngsters out that are coming up with the disease. I don't think there's anything that can be done for my wife now on the horizon. I think I just get a real good feeling of doing something for others.

The interviewer then asked whether volunteering was like working. Mr. Canfield's response suggested that yes, there were similarities, but there were also differences. It is up to the volunteer to decide what he will do and when he will do it. Doing volunteer work is doing an organization a favor. You fit it into your schedule. You do it when you can.

I feel as though you're not under a time schedule like you would be working for somebody else. Volunteering for the association, if I'm not there at ten o'clock, I get there at ten thirty, or quarter of eleven, no big deal. I'm not under any time constraints to do anything.

Mr. Canfield's wife was listening to our interview and said:

If you don't want to do it, you can say no.

Mr. Canfield responded:

Right. My time is my own. If I get up in the morning and the sun's out shining and I want to take off to the country, I'm going to go and take off to the country. And you can do things at your own pace. In some cases, sometimes there are deadlines to meet, self-imposed deadlines that you'd like to get this mailing out by noontime, so you crunch to get it done. So there are times when you work under the gun. But that's not very often.

Some among the retired have both part-time work and voluntary activities. Although Mr. Marquis worked nearly half-time, he also served on the board of an institution that provided services for his handicapped son. His board service was important in a different way from his work: the board service allowed him to feel that he was giving something back to an institution to which he felt indebted; it was reciprocity for the help the institution had given his son. Although he liked the company for which he worked, the work was his side of a market exchange: the company wanted his services and he wanted the pay. (Mr. Marquis did not actually need the pay to meet his bills but being paid established that what he did was worthwhile.)

Some voluntary activities are like the Canfields' in that the activities absorb a good deal of time, but most do not.[9] A typical volunteer might give two to four hours a week. But a retiree committed to using his or her time for volunteer work can find activities that together will absorb much of the week.

Before his retirement, one of our respondents, Mr. Abbott, had worked as a consultant to foreign firms doing business in the United States. Even then he had been active as a volunteer in his church. On his retirement he became more active still. It made him feel good to be helpful to others.

I have been able to become more involved with church work now because I have more time. I enjoy it. I've always felt if someone, within reason, said, "We have a need; will you help?" I'd try to make a time allocation and say, "Sure, we'll figure it in."

I happen to be on the ushering group of our church right now. And if someone says, "I need a ride," I do it. So there have been three women, and I sort of made the rounds to pick them up for services on Sunday. Now someone else is taking one of the women, so I'm taking the other two. If there's some maintenance work to be done at the church, I get involved in that. We have a yearly fair and I serve in that.

Those are types of things that I'm quite willing to do to be supportive of maintaining the church body as a mechanism for being of meaning to others. If people aren't prepared to volunteer, the services of the church suffer.

The church was only the first of several organizations to which Mr. Abbott contributed time. Through the church Mr. Abbott became acquainted with programs for feeding the hungry. He volunteered for occasional service with a program that required that he help prepare and hand out food and also for occasional service with Meals on Wheels.

I do some volunteer work at an organization that feeds hungry people. Some of the churches and some of the organizations rotate through, so it isn't an onerous kind of thing. It's preparing the food and handing it out.

I did Meals on Wheels today. I only substitute for Meals on Wheels. They had a little trouble understanding this. I said to them, "When you need someone, call me." Sometimes I don't get a call for three weeks; sometimes I make three deliveries in a week. I visited with a gal today who had just broken her leg and she felt very much confined. We chatted a little bit. I can't spend much time with her, but I'm appreciative of the fact that I might be the only one she'll talk to during the day.

Mr. Abbott was also a member of several veterans groups and sometimes did volunteer work for them.

I've been a participant in programs in the veterans association. I'm in charge of publicity and internal communication. With the help of the postal people, I worked out how to get the third-class mail together. We get two or three thousand pieces together. I'm the one that gets that organized and out.

Mr. Abbott liked volunteering because it permitted him to be helpful to institutions and causes he cared about, and yet remain in control of his time. He was insistent on keeping time free for his children and grandchildren. When the organizers of Meals on Wheels wanted to list him on their schedule of people who would deliver meals, Mr. Abbott reminded them sharply that he did not want to give them that much time. An advantage of volunteering over part-time work is that it gives the retiree control of his or her time.[10]

Mr. Abbott's wife was also an active volunteer. That made it easier for Mr. Abbott to maintain his own high level of effort.

My wife has done the same thing. Every other week my wife takes three women—amazing, they're eighty-five to ninety—to shop. Takes them to the supermarket.

Occasionally Mr. Abbott joined his wife in her voluntary activity.

This week I went with her because it was so slippery. It worked out beautifully. They needed a strong arm to kind of get them from the house to the car and from the car to the store.

Volunteer work can provide retirees with reassurance that they continue to be useful members of the social world. And, as volunteers, they are in control of how much they will do and when they will do it. They are, after all, doing a favor.

Organized Programs and Other Structured Social Arrangements

Organized programs make available to retirees membership in ongoing groups that are both structured and sociable. Such programs include exercise classes and college programs for learning in retirement, courses in arts and crafts held in local high schools, senior center activities, investment clubs, book groups, hiking clubs, and bridge associations. Some organized programs, such as college programs, are maintained by well-established organizations. Others, such as book groups, are organized by friends and maintained by the participants themselves.

By scheduling regular social activities focused on a common interest, organized programs provide ready-made communities to retirees. Join a book group or investment club and you obtain membership in its community of interest. Although it can take a bit of time before you are fully accepted—perhaps three or four weeks—you can count on then having a place.

Organized programs provide participants with still others of the benefits associated with work. The scheduling of the activities helps structure time just as work would: exercise classes provide a morning destination, a bridge group an activity scheduled at a particular time on a particular weekend evening.

Participation can enhance feelings of worth. In most organized programs some level of interest or ability is required for admission, although the level may vary from that of beginner to that of expert. Participation ordinarily fosters improvement in whatever skills are prized by the group. And feelings of worth can be further enhanced as competent performance is recognized and applauded.[11]

For some participants in organized programs the activities themselves are so important that the associated sociability is an annoyance. They are there to paint or dance or play bridge. They are good at whatever the activity is, may be getting better, and like having their skill recognized. They may be seen by other participants in the program as especially serious in their devotion to the activity, perhaps too much so.

Most among the retired, in most settings of organized programs, value at least as highly as the activities themselves the sociability that is made possible by regular meetings in a structured setting. Mrs. Oliver, the former office manager who overcame her social isolation, joined a potting class at a senior center primarily for its sociability. She also, for a time, participated in a potting class whose members were more single-minded in their focus on potting, but after a bit decided it was not for her. Here she first describes the more sociable class and then, briefly, and disparagingly, the other.

In our potting group, some of them are neighbors that I've known for years. No one does much work. We could care less whether we get anything done.

We just came out to have a good time. That's the only reason we're there. We pay three dollars a lesson. It's our three-dollar therapy lesson.

We do a lot of talking, a lot of laughing. A lot of craziness—we can say things to each other. No one's feelings get hurt. For instance, one woman there was saying, "Well, I'm going to be a great-grandmother." And we said, "Congratulations." And she said, "It would have been nicer if the wedding came first." And we said, "Worse things could happen." And she said, "You know, you're right."

The same teacher has Wednesday morning Potting for Seniors. And on Wednesday mornings those seniors don't talk. And like if you sit in somebody's seat—"That's my seat! Don't sit in that!"—And "I was using that! Let me have that!" And being cranky and irritable. And everything has to be perfect.

Membership in the small community of Mrs. Oliver's more friendly potting group gave rise to social events that paralleled those of the social life of an office. There was the same exchange of personal stories, the same opportunities for mutual support, and the same small dramas of interaction that enlivened the day.

In our potting group I am with women my age but I am not with complainers. Sometimes women my age can be a bunch of complainers, and I don't want to deal with that. Fortunately, the group I'm with don't want to deal with that either. So no one ever complains about pains or aches or anything. The conversation isn't about illness or anything like that. It's all about, I don't know, sometimes people might tell you something that's going on in their life. But it is not misery.

Everybody has a problem. One has a child that's severely retarded. I think he's like forty or something. Another woman has a child who is clinically depressed. Everybody is dealing with different issues in their life.

But they are just so funny. I mean, one girl took and opened a thing of paint and got it all over her. And some people would have been very upset about that. And we all start laughing and saying, "Oh, boy, now you're going to be able to go shopping and buy something new."

I guess it's the way you view things. And we can laugh over that. I mean the girl that had the paint all over her, she couldn't stop laughing. I know it's a stupid thing to laugh about, but we thought that was funny that she did that. And there she was, ready to run out and buy a new outfit. Here's a good reason to buy something new, right? This is no good anymore.

Some organized programs, including lecture courses, do not provide opportunity for the retiree's participation. Lectures can be enjoyed as entertainment, just as a movie or a play might. So a retiree might audit a course on Joyce, sitting in an audience of fellow students. There may be moments of pleasure, but the experience is social only in that others are also present.

For attendance within an organized group to provide a sense of membership, there must be active participation. It is others' acceptance, within a system of give-and-take, that conveys membership in a community. Indeed, sitting in a class without having contact with other students can reinforce a sense of social isolation.

The experience of Mr. Wilcox, a former manager of a family firm, suggests how simple attendance differs from participation. Mr. Wilcox had been fifty-nine when he left his position as manager of the firm. Rather than look for another managerial position, he bought commercial property that provided an income. Mr. Wilcox thereupon considered himself retired and looked around for something to do. He tried university courses. Although the courses were sometimes interesting, they did not work.

I took a lot of courses. The university has this seniors program, but somehow or other I didn't stay with that. I did it for photography and then I tried one or two others and it didn't click.

I tried extension courses, but I didn't enjoy them. I didn't have to take the exams and I didn't have to do the papers, so I didn't. I did do the reading, but even if I hadn't, it wouldn't have mattered. And a lot of the stuff I read I didn't bother to remember. And I didn't do it very intensely. It was passive; it was sort of like watching television almost—a little more stimulating because I liked the subject matter. But there were no demands put on me.

I didn't even have to get there if I didn't want to. A friend of mine, who got me involved in it in the first place, if the weather was bad he never showed up.

What was wrong was that Mr. Wilcox was not linked to the program or to others in the program. He was not a student. He was just a member of an audience.

Mr. Wilcox felt emotionally engaged only at those times when he became an active participant. And yet his brief experiences of participation made him more acutely aware of his outsiderness.

When I had the opportunity to speak, I'd have quite an interesting dialogue with the professor because I was at a different level. My experience was quite different from the other students'. But I had to be very careful because I wasn't really a paying student and I couldn't take up their time.

An organized program provides a sense of membership in a community only as the retiree acts as a member and is assured of others' acceptance. Talking with fellow participants before or after a college class can do some of this, but Mr. Wilcox's experience suggests that it is not enough. A more active role in the organized program is necessary.

Hobbies, Games, and Sports

A majority of respondents reported giving time to a hobby or game or sport. Hobbies included, among others, sewing, making furniture, photography, music, and investing. The only game that our respondents reported as having become the sort of engaging interest that would deserve the term "hobby" was bridge. Sports included, of course, golf, and also, though less frequently, tennis.

All these activities could be absorbing and deeply satisfying,[12] so much so that they might become central to the organization of retirees' lives. A couple of respondents did this with photography. Another respondent, formerly the owner of an electronics repair firm, gave his days to making fine furniture. (His is the exemplary retirement of chapter 8.) A retired lawyer who was also an expert golfer organized his life around golf, playing and practicing, arranging foursomes, and helping in a pro shop. A retired couple were serious enough about tennis to spend two or three hours on the court most mornings. A respondent whose marriage was in some ways unsatisfying had become immersed in the world of serious bridge players.

For others, hobbies were important and valued, but were only one activity among others. A couple were in process of becoming serious bridge players, taking lessons and participating in local tournaments, but they also traveled and had much else happening in their lives.

To be sure, not all retirees' efforts to integrate a hobby into their lives proved successful. Much depended on the fit between the activity and the person. A retiree might try a book group and then drop out for lack of interest, or return to a once cherished stamp collection only to discover that it was now a bore. Satisfactory retirement hobbies seemed to have these characteristics:

Retirees could lose themselves in the activity. The activity provided opportunity for Csikszentmihalyi's flow,[13] an absorption so complete that self-awareness is suspended.

The activity required skill. Retirees could be proud of their competence.

The activity was stress free and might be relaxing. Despite the activity's importance for the retired person, its pursuit was easy, without tension, and led to no irksome obligations.

Skill in performance of the activity or the worth of finished products produced opportunities for recognition. In games and sports skill could be demonstrated by results: one could win, or at least do well. The products of craft hobbies could be admired by friends.

Mrs. Oliver, whose description of her experience in her potting class suggested that although she liked the class she had a limited investment in throwing pots, was deeply invested in sewing. She could lose herself in it, was proud of her skill, and was gratified by others' admiration for her creations.

I find sewing very creative—and very relaxing and fulfilling. I listen to music all the while I am sewing. I love show tunes. My best time, I think, is when I am in my sewing room and I am sewing something that I am really enjoying making and there is some wonderful music on.

I do love sewing. You just take a piece of cloth and you take a pattern, and it takes a little thinking, a little skill; it keeps the brain going. And when, after you've done this, you look and you see, you say, God, look at that, that's really something.

I make most of the grandchildren's clothes and I make some things for myself. And my daughter is single and I make most of her clothes for the office. So I keep myself very busy.

Although Mrs. Oliver was alone when she produced clothes, she was aware as she sewed that the product would have social value.

Christmas Eve we went to Mass, and my daughter-in-law and my two granddaughters were in three matching outfits that I made. And they looked so elegant. My daughter-in-law would never have spent that money for something like that. And she was so happy, and the kids were so thrilled. One of them is in the choir, and the choirmaster was telling her how lovely she looked. And I just get so much out of that, that when I am making them, it is like I know that this creation is going to bring a lot of happiness.

I have made some elegant clothes for the kids that they would never have had otherwise. I never had anything growing up. And my own daughter, I couldn't afford some of the material I can now, that these girls can have now. My own daughter, I sewed for her out of necessity, but now I am sewing for pleasure. And there's a difference.

I made the flower girl dresses for my son's wedding, for my two grand-daughters and the other little flower girl. And I made my outfit for the wedding. And that day, seeing those girls coming down that aisle with those on, they looked better than the ones that the bridesmaids had that they paid a fortune for. And I just felt really good that day. Everybody was raving about the dresses. Lots of folks came up. I couldn't believe it. The photographer wanted to take a picture of the four of us together. And my best friend from childhood was the priest at the wedding, and he kept saying, "Marie, I never knew you had that in you."

Sewing was also a respite and a retreat that provided an escape from daily stresses. Becoming absorbed in a hobby can be like entering a private world.

I don't ever get to be alone. And I think that's why I really like to be alone. My husband's home all the time. We're both retired and so there is never any alone time except when I'm in there. I have converted one of my children's bedrooms into a sewing room. There was a sign, "No Admittance," there. Everybody understands. I just had to do it. I just felt like I need space; I need time to be alone. And that is when I'm happy.

It was important to Mrs. Oliver that her sewing remained stress free. To sew for income would have turned her hobby into a job.

Different people ask me to sew this or sew that. And I refuse to, because I don't want it to be a job. I don't want it ever to be a chore, because then it wouldn't be an enjoyment for me anymore. I want to do it when I am creating and getting something very positive out of it.

In retirement people can give relaxed time to activities they once wedged into the time that remained after meeting responsibilities to work and family. Now they have time for matting photographs, for making music, for cooking or pottery or mornings on the golf course.

Not all hobbies worked for all respondents. After health concerns led to his retirement, Mr. Marquis, the former businessman, decided a hobby would serve as an outlet for his restless energy. He developed a hobby in the same systematic way he had developed his business. Someone suggested a coin collection. He bought a hundred thousand pennies in which to search for rarities.

I bought about a thousand dollars, literally a thousand dollars, worth of pennies. And I looked and looked until my fingers—I've got arthritic fingers, and they got so numb. And I thought, this is ridiculous. I didn't care. If I found a penny that was worth ten dollars, big deal.

Mr. Marquis also tried stamp collecting, but he had no interest in it. He decided that no retirement hobby could have the same meaning as work. He had been accustomed when running a business to dealing with issues that affected others' lives. It was then that he called his former competitor to ask for a job.

But for many respondents hobbies did contribute significantly to their contentment with retirement. The following are some of their experiences:

Mr. Mitchell, retired inventory manager, on photography:

About a year and a half ago the senior center was having a banquet, and they were asking for donations as prizes so that people would buy a door prize ticket that would go to helping fund the center. So I donated a picture as a door prize to be given away. The people at the center said to me, "Do you have other pictures like that?" I said, "I've got about ten pictures already made up, and a few hundred slides." So they asked me if I'd like to put on a show for the center. So I put on a show with pictures and slides. I had pictures on chairs and I showed off my slides.

People were thrilled. I enjoyed it from the standpoint that it provided some recognition of my work and that people could actually say they enjoyed it.

Mrs. Gilbert, retired bookkeeper, on painting:

I was good at painting when I was a little girl. The only thing is in my days they didn't have guidance counselors. No one ever said to me, "Why don't you go to art school?" I didn't do that until my kids were little and I needed a day out away from them. And I started out with china painting. Someone was going to a china painting class and said, "Want to join me?" I loved it. That's what started my interest in painting.

I've got some beautiful things I did in china painting. I have given my daughter a lot of my china paintings because those things are really special. She loves that stuff.

Mr. Fletcher, the former real-estate broker, on genealogy:

Since the genealogical society is a couple of blocks away, I used to go there quite often, do some research. It was convenient. It's something that I've taken up in my old age. It's sort of fun. It's detailed and it's accurate, and you can make charts and things like that. You have one name that hasn't been traced before in some book and then you have a whole load of ancestry that goes way back to England, and that opens up a whole new branch of people. So you got a whole bunch of new names. It's detailed desk work, record keeping, that I enjoy. It's something that's so definite.

No one else is interested except for nephews and nieces. But you get it down on paper—which I'm always getting it down on paper—that's always sort of fun. And there is a sense of accomplishment, I guess.

Retirees can find in hobbies support for feelings of competence and opportunities for achievement that they had previously found in their jobs. Part-time work and organized programs can also provide these, but hobbies have one distinctive advantage. Hobbies can be picked up or dropped at will. They are always available, no matter how odd the hour, and they can be put away whenever they lose their appeal. They are rewarding activities that in no way constrain retirement's freedom.

Travel

Part-time work, volunteering, organized programs, and hobbies all partially replace the provisions of work. Travel can also do this: competence is required to arrange a trip and to ensure that it goes well, and achievement is demonstrated by returning with photographs to display. But travel, more than other activities, celebrates retirement's freedom from obligation.

Being able to travel can seem almost the essence of retirement: if you are retired, and only if you are retired, you can travel whenever you want, for however long you want. When people worked, they may have traveled on business or during vacations, but either way the job dictated when they went and how long they stayed. In retirement the timing and duration of travel are limited only by family obligations, which are likely to be negotiable; health, which usually is good enough; and disposable income.

Those anticipating retirement often associate retirement with travel. Asked what they will do when they retire, many prospective retirees list travel among their first thoughts, whether or not they actually have plans to travel. And unquestionably, the idea of travel is attractive to new retirees. In some ways anticipation of travel plays the role that an anticipated vacation might have played during their years of work. It is something to look forward to, a promise of a break in routine, a time of escape from the expectations of others.

For some, travel immediately after retirement plays the role of a rite of passage, marking the end of one way of life and the beginning of another.[14] A "big trip" can be an effective way to celebrate entrance into a phase of life from which the imperatives of work have disappeared. It can provide a time out in which to take stock and give thought to the future. Travel, used this way, is like a retreat. It is an opportunity for contemplation.[15]

There are, of course, many reasons for travel, including those in which the travel is incidental to escaping the snow, seeing the kids, visiting friends, or attending a memorial service. But travel for travel's sake, just to see new places and have new experiences, is what people contemplating retirement generally have in mind when they say that they hope to travel.

Sometimes people have promised themselves a trip once they have the time. A former physician among our respondents drove across the country with his wife, his wife's sister, and her husband, making major stops for the Grand Canyon and New Orleans. He had always wanted to do that, and retirement made it possible. He was elated by the trip's utter freedom from responsibility, demonstrated by the group's ability to decide, day by day, where they would go next and how long they would stay.

Many couples find that planning a big trip provides a shared activity at a time when they might otherwise become immersed in their separate lives. Planning for the trip requires that they agree on dates and places. Taking the trip requires that they work together to make it all go well. Later, after they have returned from the trip, they have an important shared experience they can together talk about to others.

Especially for those who did not do much traveling earlier in their lives, travel brings firsthand contact with the larger world. Think of a parade whose route has taken it not by your home but rather a couple of streets away. Unless you are told, "It wasn't worth watching," your reaction is apt to be disappointment. You missed it. You could be told about the parade in exquisite detail, but the more the description makes the parade sound like fun, the greater your regret for not having seen it. Travel is seeing the attraction. It is being there.

People return from travel with stories of having seen the Taj Mahal, the Acropolis, the Blarney Stone, the Great Wall of China. They may bring back photographs, but the photographs are as much testimonies to their having actually been there as they are reminders of what they saw. And travel has done more than simply permit them to see an object: it has provided that object with a context of surrounding space, of people met in getting to it and joined in witnessing it, of the whole experience of traveling to get to the object's site and of living, for a time, in its setting.[16]

Travel involves a testing of oneself. Simply getting oneself to this foreign place requires some doing. Once there, the traveler must meet challenges: finding a place to stay, getting tickets for a play or ballet or sporting event, obtaining a railroad schedule and then mastering it. A good restaurant may seem doubly good if it is the culmination of a success story: obtaining its name from a concierge and then checking its quality with a local acquaintance, deciphering the bus system and getting off at the right place, actually finding the restaurant, and then prevailing on the person at the door to provide a table.

Encounters with new people, if they go even reasonably well, count as good travel experiences. When retirees reminisce about their travel experience, it is the challenges they surmounted and the people they met that count, perhaps more than the art and the castles and the scenery.[17]

Travelers also encounter themselves. One of the attractions of travel is that a new situation, with new people, provides opportunity to express a self ordinarily submerged in the routine back home. At the same time, as the accustomed self emerges to cope with the challenges of travel, there is the chance to see it in relief, to appreciate its strengths, and, usually without penalty, to recognize its shortcomings.

Traveling can be done at any level of challenge. Retirees can choose tours in which the tour operator assumes responsibility for transportation, meals, hotels, and experiences. Or they can backpack on their own, using local maps and taking their chances on places to sleep. Our respondents almost invariably chose levels of challenge with which they felt comfortable. Many reported unexpected problems they had to deal with, but few reported bad travel experiences.

Mrs. Walker had been the financial manager of the retail outlet of a large electronics firm. She was forced into retirement when her firm was sold and the new owners closed the outlet. For years she had envied married friends who had the freedom and funds for travel.

I've been widowed twenty-six years. I was left with four little children. And I went to work, and you come home and you take care of a house and four kids and school and all the things that you have to do and one car, and you're busy. And I never felt sorry for myself, but I know that there were many things that my friends had, because fortunately they had their spouses, and I'm happy for them. They've traveled, and I would have liked to have gone and traveled, and

I couldn't. I haven't been unhappy about it, but I've been aware of it all my life. Until my kids all went out of the house, I had a great deal of responsibility, so I couldn't travel. I think, over the years, I haven't felt sorry for myself, but I felt a little cheated that were things different, I could have enjoyed some of these other things.

Now retired and with both time and discretionary income for the first time since her husband died, Mrs. Walker could give herself the travel she had so long envied her friends for having. In addition, she suspected that if she did not travel now, she might never.

I'm at this point in my life when I say, forget it, it's later than you think. If you don't take advantage of it, there's a point at which you're not going to be able to take advantage of it. Maybe you're not going to be here or physically you're not going to be able to go, or who knows what's going to happen. We never know what tomorrow's going to be. So I want to try to take advantage of whatever opportunity presents itself. I want to try and get it in now if I can and if it's within my financial means.

A friend invited Mrs. Walker to join a tour of New Orleans. She accepted. The travel turned out to be as gratifying as she had always thought it would be.

It was wonderful. It's a real fun city. We walked around every day. We were out at the crack of dawn in our sneakers and our running suits. And we just went all over the French Quarter, and just saw a great deal of New Orleans.

We went to Preservation Hall for three shows. We wouldn't leave. And the wonderful restaurants. Just the atmosphere. The freedom. It was right before Halloween, and the place of course was crowded. And I guess it had much of a Mardi Gras atmosphere, because people were walking around in costumes, and everything was decorated, and wherever you walked the music was blasting out of these places. And it was such a gay, happy, fun place, everything about it. I just loved it. It was loose; it was easy; it was laid-back.

Mrs. Walker was pleased to have had no more challenge than the level presented by a tour. She had enough time on her own to feel unrestricted and at the same time she enjoyed being looked after.

It's so easy; everything's taken care of for you—the transportation and the dinner plans and your theater tickets. And they had a wonderful itinerary planned. We went to many historical places, wonderful restaurants.

I'm perfectly capable of writing away for theater tickets and calling the airport and making my reservations. And I like to take care of myself. I am terribly independent. I've been forced to be independent. But it's nice being taken care of, having these details taken care of. I like that. And we did a lot on our own.

The tour made Mrs. Walker determined to travel more. She felt herself richer for having taken it. And she had only so much time left to see more and to learn more.

You know, time's growing short, so I don't want to go back to the same place forty times. I want to go to a new place each time to get the flavor and the interest, the education, everything.

Others among our respondents also said they were determined to travel before aging or illness made travel impossible. One respondent said her parents had waited too long to travel and so never did. She scheduled a trip for herself to begin immediately after her retirement.

Yet not everyone who retires wants to travel. Those who had traveled extensively as part of their jobs might now think of retirement as an opportunity to stay home. One respondent who felt this way very strongly was Mr. Abbott, the former international consultant who gave so much time to volunteer activity. He had traveled constantly for his work; he had no desire ever to travel again.

What do I want to do in retirement? I don't want to travel. I have no interest in traveling at all, because I traveled for business extensively. I want to develop the estate so that it's more attractive. I might even attempt to extend my knowledge in the area of taxes and things like that. But I'm not turned on to travel. How many trips do you take before it palls on you? What's the point?

Travel, for most people, requires companionship. Experiences are richer if shared. More than that, being alone among strangers can exacerbate feelings of loneliness and social isolation. Most people need others with whom to agree on destinations and with whom to talk at dinner. A companion's response to a shared experience helps deepen one's own. It may also be easier to allow oneself to be captured by new experience if one has the security of a companion. Some solitary travelers are happy not to have to compromise their itineraries to please someone else, and are willing to put up with occasional loneliness if that is the cost of their independence. But the majority of travelers feel that traveling goes best with a companion.

Mrs. Walker, for example, believed herself fortunate to have had a friend to travel with. In the future, she said, traveling on a tour might be acceptable, but she would not travel alone.

I was very fortunate that I went with my friend because she's a real go-go person. And we just enjoy the same things.

I might have gone alone if I didn't have an option. And I might in the future if someone doesn't want to go with me. But I wouldn't go alone, alone. Traveling with a group, yeah, because when you go and you see how friendly people are, and they kind of gather you in, it's very nice. And you don't have to be alone.

Mr. Hindes, the widowed former manager, gave as one reason for his remarriage his desire for a companion with whom he could travel. This was far from his only reason, but it did play a role in his thinking.

I wanted to have a life, a new life. I wanted a house. I wanted to have a wife. I probably needed commitment. I had it for thirty-five years, so it wasn't something new to me. I wanted to share the rest of my life with somebody. I don't know how else I could put it.

I wanted to share. My wife isn't there anymore. I couldn't share the sunset with anybody. I couldn't share anything. And you don't travel alone. I wanted to travel. And I wanted to share with somebody. Now if I want to go to the country on a vacation, I have a partner to share it with. I have a partner to plan it with. I have a partner to enjoy it with. I have a partner to remember it with.

Limited finances did not seem to make travel impossible. Retirees who were not able to spend a great deal on travel were able to travel to destinations reachable by car. They might camp rather than stay in a hotel, and eat by the side of the road or in their rooms rather than in restaurants. They might visit the kids a hundred miles along the high-way rather than take an expensive tour to Europe. But, like other re-tirees, now that they had the time to get away, they found a way to do it. And, again like other retirees, they seemed generally to enjoy the trip.

Puttering

The weekdays of retirees frequently begin slowly. There is a leisurely breakfast during which the newspaper is read cover to cover. A sec-ond cup of coffee may be poured to accompany the crossword puzzle. The morning may be well on its way before the breakfast dishes are collected and thought is given to the day ahead. Before their retire-ment, retirees would have left for work Mondays through Fridays. They would have given Saturday mornings to errands and chores, and only on Sunday mornings would they have lingered through breakfast until, among churchgoers, it was time for church. In retirement every morning can be Sunday morning.

Ms. Putnam, the former college administrator, described how the start of her day had changed since her retirement.

I still am up and showered and dressed and get the newspaper by eight o'clock just about every morning. The difference is I now sit with the news-paper—read it, do the crossword puzzle, have a second cup of coffee. And then about ten o'clock start off with what I'm going to do for the day.

Retirees tend to prize these relaxed morning hours. They find plea-sure in the absence of appointments and in being able to extend their breakfast as they wish. Mr. Crittenden, the former financial institution executive, described sharing this sort of morning with his wife.

It takes me three hours to get up in the morning. I read two newspapers thoroughly. It gets a little out of kilter in the summertime when I leave early to play golf or something, just enough to give it a little variety. Generally in the winter, it's almost without exception: we spend from six-thirty to nine-thirty eating breakfast and reading the paper. From six-thirty to nine-thirty is a very nice part of our day.

Puttering is a relaxed way of moving through a day, engaging in activities as they attract one's attention, undertaking nothing that demands energy and concentration. The dishes need doing, so why not do them now? It's nice out, and a bit of gardening might be enjoyable. It's noontime; make a sandwich and watch the news on television. Later, put the newspaper away and pick up the magazines that somebody carried into the front room. Straighten the room. Pick up a book and do a bit of reading. Start the computer and check e-mail. Think about organizing the attic. Nothing has special urgency.

Retirees seem not to be bored by puttering. There is always something with which to fill time. The puttering is regularly interrupted by an activity to attend, a hobby to look at, a walk or a bit of shopping or a break for coffee with a friend. Mr. Oldsten was among respondents who rather liked taking it easy. He had been purchasing director for a high-tech company, a job that was frequently stressful. His wife was still employed and so he spent most of the day alone.

Yesterday I got up, had some breakfast. I went out for about three or four hours and did a little bit of window-shopping. I got back around noontime or so. I had lunch, watched the news, then just puttered around the house. We had supper and watched television for a while. We usually go to bed around nine or ten o'clock; last night it was ten o'clock. Very unexciting, very uneventful.

I can sit down and do absolutely nothing for an hour. And it doesn't bother me. I enjoy a chance to relax and not have the pressure of having to do something.

And here is how Mr. Paige, the former computer engineer, described his use of time.

Today the big event was to clean out the freezer down cellar and scrape the ice off of it and make a list of what is in there so my wife'll know what's there. I did a little reading, read the newspaper of course. I watch the news every day. I had planned to take a walk, which I may do yet if the spirit moves. I like to walk. I'll probably go out and at least walk around the block, which is a mile and a quarter or two miles, depending on which way I go.

Yesterday I did some work around the house but I don't remember what it was. We have a stove in the back, and I think I cleaned that out. Wood stove. I worked on that. I did some reading.

If I make up my mind to do something, I do it at my own speed. I told my wife one thing I wanted to do is I want to go through the house top to bottom and touch everything I own, and if I don't need it, get rid of it. So far I've only done the attic.

Part of Mr. Paige's previous day had been given to a project that seemed worthwhile but for which he might not have had time when he worked. Again, there was no sense of urgency.

One thing I did yesterday, we're kind of thinking of getting a new car, and I spent some time making up lists of different cars and prices and so on in the size range and the price range that we're interested in, to get some comparison.

In the evening, as retirees look back on a day of puttering, they may feel that it had gone by quickly, possibly just because it was so nearly featureless, so lacking in the charged events and encounters that had crowded the days of their employment. And yet a day of puttering can seem to have been full, filled with slow-paced activities closely following one after another. Some retireees joked that they couldn't understand how they had ever had time for work.

Mrs. Norwell, herself newly retired from a publishing firm, was surprised at her husband's contentment with days that, aside from a hobby, were spent mostly in puttering.

He's been retired for ten years. He's a retired architect and he sits on juries occasionally. But that doesn't involve terribly much. He builds a lot of ship models. He does a lot of crossword puzzles. Sometimes he reads. And otherwise he just sits in his chair. He doesn't watch TV till evening. He does crossword puzzles, reads, and is perfectly happy.

Some retirees try to schedule tasks for their days. They may begin with a list of things to be done, though one problem with lists is the ease with which they are mislaid. In other cases, retirees sometimes make a brave start moving through items on their lists, but then the puttering mode takes over. Mr. Foster, the former lawyer, was among retirees who tried to impose a structure on their time. His success in getting everything done was mixed.

What I usually do, my normal routine, usually, is to get up in the morning, have a cup of coffee, get my engine started, and then make a list of things that I want to get done that day. Yesterday's list had lots of items on it. There was a stop at the church, tend to some business there, shopping, fix a chair. I spent quite a bit of time yesterday taking apart and redoing a chair – little stuff like that around the house. I do some work downstairs, carpentry work, or whatever, a few projects. I've got a dollhouse I'm going to make for my grandchild.

I find that I've almost too much to do. In the last few months I've found that at the end of the day I didn't get everything done that I wanted to get done. That's okay. I'd much rather have it that way than be sitting around trying to think of things to do.

One problem in puttering is that the retiree can feel that he or she isn't really doing anything and so ought to be available to others in the family. Relatives who live nearby may call on the retired person to look after the kids or to check on the house, and the retired person will feel required to say yes, of course. Mrs. Aubrey, herself about to retire from an administrative position in town government, said this was the case with her husband, a former electrical engineer.

Last week my husband got a call from our daughter-in-law. His one-year-old granddaughter was sick, and Mommy had to go to work, and would somebody come and babysit? Well, I had to go to work too, so he went. That was about four hours.

For Mr. Aubrey it was a day well spent. He could look after his granddaughter, was able to talk with his son, and did some reading. But even if he had not wanted to baby-sit, Mr. Aubrey could not have refused to help out. Given the pervasiveness of Ekerdt's "busy ethic," in which the time of retirement ought to be used actively, he could not give any importance to his puttering.[18]

Chapter Seven

Marriage and Family

As people move on in life, they follow increasingly divergent paths. Most, but not all, marry; among those who marry, some celebrate anniversary after anniversary whereas others divorce and still others face bereavement. Some have children; some do not.[1]

The quality of retirement is heavily affected by the life path that led to it. There is, of course, much else that matters: health, wealth, previous work, and how that work was left. But of first importance may be the retiree's life situation. The retirement of those who live alone is at risk of persisting social isolation. The same is true, although to a lesser extent, of the retirement of those whose partner remains employed. If both partners are retired, much depends on the extent to which the partnership is happy.

A married retiree whose spouse will also be at home full time enters a situation unprecedented in their married lives. During their years of work the husband and wife would have been separated from each other from morning to evening, Monday through Friday. Now, if they wish, they can be in each other's company all through the day on weekdays as well as weekends. They can read the morning paper together, shop together, cook together, and watch the evening news together. Each can be available to the other throughout the day to help with a chore or supply a phone number or listen to an account of a phone call just completed.

Some couples are pleased by the prospect of so much time together.

Others worry that it will be entirely too much. Should they choose to be together through the days, they may see less of their friends, and, instead, much more of each other. They will be subject to the other's surveillance and called on to respond to the other's concerns. Their phone calls will no longer be private. Indeed, very little will be private.

At the same time that retirement makes it possible for couples to be together more, it strengthens a change that may already have shown itself in the marriage. Most retired couples live by themselves in their homes, the youngest of their children having already left for adulthood. Without children to care for, they have less need to make the logistics of homemaking their first priority. Instead they can simply enjoy each other's company. Marital companionship benefits from retirement.

On the other hand, some marriages have found a comfortable balance of togetherness and separation that is threatened by retirement. Marital unhappiness can make retirement positively unattractive; the prospect of more time at home can slow the movement into retirement of unhappily married husbands and wives. But it is not unusual for even happily married couples to have a bit of trepidation when they consider the change in their lives that retirement will bring.

Dr. Metcalf, the former research scientist, said that his wife, who was still working, was worried about the increased togetherness that would occur when she too retired:

She's not too sure how it's going to work when she's retired. She doesn't know if she can stand being in the same place with me all day long. It was just one of those casual conversations; we were talking about it. It was said half jokingly: "I don't know whether I can stand you all day long." But it could be a problem.

A husband or wife who had been a stay-at-home spouse for some time, perhaps having retired earlier, may have a number of concerns about sharing the home during the workweek. Might the retiring partner require constant attention?[2] Some wives who had been out of the workforce for a while worried that their husbands would want their lunch prepared for them. They might quote the remark "I agreed to 'for better or for worse.' I didn't agree to 'for lunch.'"[3]

Wives who had been out of the labor force when their husbands retired were aware of the belief that retired husbands are intrusive, applying energies no longer absorbed by work to alphabetizing the spice shelves. A male retiree said that his wife had been asked by her friends, "Has he rearranged the kitchen yet?" The husband wondered if his wife had any special reason for telling him.[4]

Husbands who had been at home for a while when their wives retired were not worried that they would be expected to prepare lunch for the wives. But they did sometimes worry that their wives would want them to be ever-present companions. They might insist, when their wives actually did retire, that they would nevertheless retain their previous routines.

Husbands and wives who were the first to retire, and were home alone while their spouses worked, might discover another kind of discomfort: days alone and evenings with a spouse preoccupied by work. To retire while one's spouse continues to be employed risks social isolation.

A study of a large sample of people moving into retirement found that couples tend to experience an upsurge of conflict during the first year or two after retirement. This seems to be the case whether they retire together or first one retires and then the other, but couples in which the man has retired and his wife has not may be especially prone to conflict. All couples then seem to do better with the passage of time. Fully retired couples, couples in which both husband and wife have retired, seem to do best of all. Couples in which both partners have been retired at least a couple of years report levels of conflict lower than that of couples in which husband or wife or both remain in the labor force.[5]

For a retiree without a partner, the risk of social isolation following retirement is significant. In addition, loneliness can be harder to manage without the distractions of work. Although retirement can create problems for the married, it is much more likely to create problems for people on their own.

When Both Spouses Are at Home

When both partners were retired, each seemed pleased by their increased time together. Although a bit of time might have been needed to get used to the new basis of life, the problems seemed entirely manageable. Should either need time alone, that seemed to be worked out without problems.

To a remarkable extent, retired couples can adjust the degree to which their time is shared. They can choose activities that are shared: gardening together, taking walks together, seeing movies together, playing bridge together, traveling together, and jointly planning for future travel. Or they can limit their companionship by choosing to participate in activities from which the spouse is absent: working part time, playing golf, having lunches with friends, taking courses offered by an adult education program. They can travel with friends or siblings or children rather than with each other.

Puttering can be an occupation for two. Here is Mr. Crittenden's description of his postretirement mornings.

I still wake up at six-thirty. Most of the time I'm the first one up, and I get down and put on the coffee and put on the oats. If my wife wants something special, she'll wander down and help. I'm the oats maker. And then I bring it up on a big tray, and we have breakfast together in bed, just reading the paper. We both have big night tables.

… It's a good communication time too. Generally there are articles in the paper that we comment on. This morning there was an obituary that I commented on, a British musician that we had met on one of our trips. And there was a news story my wife commented on about two sisters that were living alone and were robbed. It reinforced her belief that someone knew them and knew the house and I should be very careful if anyone comes to the door not to let them in if we don't know them.

The Crittendens' day continued in this mode of quiet companionship. This was yesterday:

About nine-thirty, quarter of ten, we finished the papers. She was doing a few things around the house and I showered and then she showered and we both got ready, and at eleven-thirty we went and did Meals on Wheels, which took us until about quarter of one.

The afternoon provided breaks from togetherness. Mr. Crittenden went to play golf, and Mrs. Crittenden napped. Before her nap Mrs.

Crittenden prepared food for dinner. Later Mr. Crittenden watched television, and Mrs. Crittenden went for a walk.

We came home and she had some things she wanted to do in the house, and I said, "Well, I'm going to get in nine holes of golf." When I came home, she was fast asleep in her afternoon nap and had made a nice batch of tuna fish. Then I guess I watched the business report or something, and she just took a walk in the neighborhood. One of our neighbors had come back from a vacation, so they were standing out in the court, chatting. We went to bed early, and I was asleep by nine-fifteen.

The Crittendens' companionship was enriched by shared interests in the arts. Together they attended performances by the local symphony, where they were season ticket holders, served on the board of directors of a music school, and, as members, visited the large art museum that was some twelve miles from their home. In addition, they both enjoyed traveling. At one point their liking for music and travel led to a week in New York City, where they attended performances of Wagner's Ring Cycle.

We have a common interest in music. We go to the symphony together. We like to travel together. We got a mailing for a week in New York, the complete Ring Cycle. She mentioned it to me and I said, "Hey, I've never had the leisure or the opportunity to sit down and go through a whole Ring Cycle in one week." So we splurged for it. We went down, and it was really a great trip.

Each had interests that the other did not share but was aware of. Mr. Crittenden valued this element of independence.

She still has a lot of activities that do not include me. She's always been active in the choral society. That gives her plenty of focus. And then she has her ladies' bridge groups. And that doesn't bother me, because I either want to golf, in good weather, or I'm doing something in my study in the afternoon. So it isn't like we need each other to get through the day.

Mr. Crittenden thought his retirement had been good for his marriage. He was more emotionally accessible. Before his retirement he had been tense before starting off for work and tired when he returned in the evening.

I think my wife enjoys my company more, in that she'll remark on something, I'll put down what I'm doing, and I'm willing to discuss that. Whereas before, if she said something to me in the morning, you know, "Geez, watch it, I'm shaving; I got to catch the train," and this sort of thing.

So I have time to have that communication with my wife that I didn't have before. Because the inner workings of, say, the church's board of directors are more interesting to me now because I have time to listen to them. Before, they sort of faded in importance. "You're going to have more outreach? Fine." And that was the end of the conversation. Now I'll take time to hear about who's doing what, and so forth.

Mr. Mathers, the former sales manager, noted a similar improvement in his relationship with his wife. Before his retirement he had been preoccupied when at home.[6]

My relationship with my wife I'd say has improved considerably. Not that we did not have a good relationship. But now I have more time to show affection towards her and be with her and to walk together and to be together more often and to be more relaxed with her. Before, every time I was with her, I had another problem in the back of my mind. Now I don't have that. Now I have the love that I really have for her and it's because there's nothing else cluttering my mind. No problems. So that's another benefit of retirement that a lot of people don't realize.

It was earlier noted that wives and husbands who had retired before their spouses, and had grown accustomed to having their homes to themselves during the workweek, were sometimes apprehensive that a soon-to-retire spouse would encroach on their freedom. Several found that a greater problem was their own sense of responsibility. Retired wives, especially, seemed to change their schedules to accommodate what they thought were the needs of their newly retired husbands. Mr. Ulrich, the former project director for a financial institution, said that was happening in his marriage.

She's a little more restricted. She hasn't admitted to it, but I don't think that she associates with her friends as much as she used to because I'm home, and I think she feels a little guilty if she's not home for my lunch. Even though I assure her not to worry about me because I can take care of myself, I know it's restricting her. And I just say, "Please call so and so and go out." And she says, "Oh, yeah, I will." And she does, sometimes.

Husbands who had retired earlier than their wives generally seemed less likely than stay-at-home wives to feel responsible for providing companionship to their newly retired spouses. A stay-at-home husband might permit his newly retired wife to take over the cooking, but dropping his golf games or his times with friends would be another matter.

Mrs. Pierce, the former marketing manager, had retired some years after her husband's disability-based departure from work. Her job had required her to travel, and she had had assignments that required that she be away from home weeks at a time. When she went on disability leave, she discovered that her husband did not want her to upset his schedule. Nor was he much help in dealing with the vulnerability to social isolation that she experienced.

When I retired I entered his domain. I was not the typical housewife. I always worked out of town. He is the one who always worked in town, I always worked out of town. He always had the house for whatever he wanted, whenever he wanted. When I came home, retired, just like that, cold turkey. And when I came home, retired, I was into his domain.

That was terrible. I was trespassing on his territory. On his time. He has a brother, they go walking every day and they do things together every day. I found myself questioning him: "Where are you going?" "What are you doing that for?" "Well, I always have." I said, "Yeah, but I'm home now. And you don't have to do that. That isn't going to happen anymore, is it?" And he said, "Of course it is going to happen."

Despite Mrs. Pierce's vulnerability to social isolation following her departure from work, she said that she felt no anger toward her husband for not being more available to her. Indeed, she believed she respected him for his insistence on maintaining his previous routine.

I had to respect that. Because I couldn't respect a man that doesn't respect his own actions. He said, "So you are home, but I have to do what I have to do." And that was great. So that was ironed out. Now we just hang loose and respect one another's needs and wants.

Some jointly retired couples established rules and understandings regarding times when they were not to be intruded on. For example, the husband was to be out of the kitchen when his wife was preparing a meal, and the wife was not to bother her husband when he was using the computer to track their investments. Occasionally a spouse attempted to establish such a rule but failed.

In one couple, the Sillers, Mrs. Siller was regularly annoyed with her husband for being in the way when she was doing housework. The Sillers had worked together and retired together. Dr. Siller had been a physician in private practice, and his wife had been his office manager. After their joint retirement they were home together most of the time. Mrs. Siller complained that her husband's presence made her tasks more difficult.

Whether a man retires or not, a woman has her work to do. I have a fairly large house here and I have my own appointments, my own things. And it's a pain in the butt to have him around in the morning. That's when I'd like to get my work done. When I go up to make the bed, I don't want anybody in it, reading the paper.

Intellectually, I realize that he really does deserve to have that rest. But emotionally it's not easy to accept. I'd like to get my work in my home done in the morning, then go out to do errands or whatever. You can't get your work done when there's someone hanging around. So I hope he will do something.

Mr. Vella, the former contractor, had been married to a stay-at-home spouse. His wife had helped out in his construction business but otherwise had never worked. When Mr. Vella retired, his wife let him know that she would be happier if he were not around the house throughout the day. He had retained some business interests—real estate, a snowplowing sideline—and he now gave them more attention.

My wife figures if I'm hanging around the house, I'm sticking my nose into the cooking or something like that, I expect. That's what she was figuring. She often says, "Well, you couldn't stay around here all day anyway. You'd drive me crazy." I think that's probably true. It hasn't happened because I'm not there.

In a few instances husband and wife seemed genuinely troubled by their increased time together. Their marriages had worked well enough when they saw each other only evenings and weekends but seemed without much basis for additional hours of companionship. Their joint retirement upset one or both of them, and they looked for ways to limit their time together. In one instance the husband went on long fishing trips by himself. In another the husband found part-time work that would get him out of the house.[7]

But for the most part, the joint retirement of a husband and wife proved beneficial for each. Along with the increased companionship, couples reported more nearly shared contributions to the home. Given the free time the husband now had, he could more easily share in the routine work of the home: shopping, cleaning, cooking. Many men, however, preferred to make their contributions to the home by performing the handyman chores of small repairs within the home and maintenance work outside the home: mowing and raking in the summer and fall and shoveling snow in the winter.[8] They were ready to help with shopping and cooking and cleaning, but it seemed that although they gave more time and attention to the home than they previously had, their wives did not give much less. Mr. Crittenden, for example, did more in the home than he had before his retirement, but his wife continued to be responsible for cooking and most housework.

We have a very good working relationship on taking care of the home. I know the bathroom floors are too hard for her now, so I have no qualms about doing it. I don't have this "women's work" and "men's work." There are some things she does better than I, other things that I'm more capable of doing. She does a lot of traditional things. Like I take care of the outside and she takes care of the inside. It just falls into that pattern.

She has a better feel for many things. And she knows where to hang the pictures better than I. She's a better cook than I am—especially with the leftovers; she can make them taste great. If I try to make a stew with everything in the refrigerator, it turns up tasting like slop. She knows her herbs and so forth. But I grill. I'm a good griller.

Despite occasional instances in which couples needed to limit their time together, being able to be with the spouse throughout the day was generally seen as one of the great benefits of dual retirements.

Retirement with a Working Spouse

For couples in which one spouse has retired while the other remains employed, the retiree is most often the man. Usually the man is older and so the first to reach retirement age. In addition, if the woman entered or reentered the labor force only after her children were school-age, she may have reached a position of influence and autonomy just when her husband was ready to end his career. Furthermore, if the woman has had only a few years of employment, she may prefer work and its new challenges to what may seem in comparison to be the quiet tedium of life at home.

Men whose wives continue to work when they themselves have retired can, if they wish, become the supportive nonworking spouse. For some men this role reversal is agreeable, for others not. Irrespective of their attitude, men who took on the supportive spouse role found themselves in situations that made for vulnerability to social isolation. They had left the social community of their work, were without membership in another community, and, if they were to reestablish such membership, would have to do it on their own.

Dr. Metcalf, the former research scientist, tried at first to be the supportive spouse for his still employed wife. He said that his wife had taken primary responsibility for their home when they both worked and now that he was retired it was only fair that he be the homemaker. He kept the house in order and did the shopping, although his wife, who both agreed was the better cook, prepared their dinner. In the evenings he talked with his wife about her problems at the office.

Three months after his retirement Dr. Metcalf said his retirement arrangement was fine. Any problems were minor:

Of course now I do much of the housework, so my wife likes that. I don't do it as well as she does it, but at least I do it. I vacuum the rugs, wash the kitchen floor, do the laundry, stuff like that. She still cooks. I clean up, though.

My wife's working doesn't bother me at all. The only time it bothers me is when we want to go on vacation and she only has two weeks and I want to go for longer. Right now her working is a problem in the timing of doing things. We have to do things on Saturday and we'd rather do them on Wednesday because there are less people driving, that sort of thing. It's not a serious problem. I don't miss her during the day. She was never there during the day.

But when we talked with Dr. Metcalf a year later, we learned that his effort to be a stay-at-home spouse had failed. The primary problem was social isolation. Dr. Metcalf became too restless to remain at home for hours on end. For a time the Metcalfs had experienced conflict over undone household chores, but then they hired help. Despite the hired help, Dr. Metcalf's problems persisted: boredom, restlessness, inexplicable depression.

I was going to do household chores and I never did. Finally my wife got pretty mad at me, and we hired somebody to do it. I was getting bored, personally. The fact that she was working didn't really bother me. That wasn't the point. The point was that I was bored. I wasn't doing very much, and life was getting dull. What is the point of all this, essentially? And then I'd suddenly get depressed about it.

Part-time work as a consultant turned out to be a cure. A friend had recommended him; Dr. Metcalf had not sought the job, had not even known about it until he was called. He said later that the job had been a lifesaver.

Mr. Hindes, the former department head in a public utility, had been widowed a few years before his retirement. He grieved for a couple of years, then began a search, ultimately successful, for someone new.

Mr. Hindes's new wife was employed full time. Taking on responsibility for managing the new household seemed to Mr. Hindes an improvement over his previous solitary life. Nor did he complain of social isolation. He was on friendly terms with the neighborhood storekeepers, and he had friends in the neighborhood whom he might bump into when he was out shopping. But most important to his mood seemed to be his enthusiasm for his home. He did not mind in the least being a househusband.

Yesterday I went out and I did shopping, errands. I went to the post office and I think I did a mailing for my wife. Kind of like a housewife.

I keep myself busy. I can't see how people don't have things to do. There's so many things you can do. We made a closet. We planned that out. I painted the whole place after they put up the ceiling. And then I put down the rugs. And, I don't know, there's so many things.

What made Mr. Hindes's attitude toward being a househusband different from Dr. Metcalf's? Mr. Hindes and his wife were much more active socially in the evening and on weekends than were the Metcalfs. That played a role. Also, Mr. Hindes's morale may have been sustained by his enthusiasm for his new marriage and his sense of himself during the day as an agent of that marriage.

The experience of another former scientist in our sample, Dr. Hamilton, also is relevant. Dr. Hamilton's wife, like Dr. Metcalf's, continued to work after Dr. Hamilton's retirement. Dr. Hamilton could not envision himself remaining home alone, waiting for his wife to return from work. He chose instead to spend most of the workweek at what had been his summer place, a farm about a hundred miles from his home. He missed his wife, but he felt more a part of things there.

We had to work out a grown-up solution to the fact that my wife is still working. I spend four days a week at our farm. It isn't convenient for my wife to go there weekends, so I come back to town. I take the bus to get back and forth. I don't drive. I've been doing that ever since I retired.

I have lots to do down there. We have a fairly large piece of land. I do a lot of outdoor work. I do a lot of gardening and landscaping. I do a lot of clearing of land, brush clearing and road building. So I'm busy. And I like being outdoors and getting plenty of physical activity.

I'm chairman of the Zoning Board of Appeals there and also I'm the secretary of the Town Affairs Council. So that gives me some challenging work to do. It has given me a chance to meet people in the community and to get to feel part of the community, not just a summer visitor or something.

I would like to spend all the time with my wife, and she with me. But the problem is I don't want to sit in the apartment all day just reading books and going out for little walks around the block. I'd find that very boring.

Another retiree whose wife worked went to Florida for the winter. There he rented an apartment near his brother's home. Once or twice during the winter his wife flew down to join him. When he asked his wife to retire so she could be with him through the winter, she said she would, but not quite yet. He did not like being in Florida alone, but he preferred it to staying north, where he would have long days alone, waiting for his wife to return from work.

Retired women, too, tend to feel uncomfortable in taking on the role of supportive spouse for a still working husband or, as was the case with Mrs. Oliver and Mrs. Pierce, a husband whose routine takes him out of the home for much of the day. Both Mrs. Oliver and Mrs. Pierce regretted having traded interesting work for the humdrum routine and relative isolation of their homes. The togetherness of couples who are both retired may have its problems, but they are generally easily remedied; the problems that stem from the separateness of couples in which only one is retired seem more difficult to remedy.

Children

Retired parents, like any parents, keep in touch with developments in their children's lives and are proud when the children do well and concerned when they do not. They stand ready to help should help be needed: to make loans or gifts to carry the children through a bad financial patch, to take the grandchildren should the children be incapacitated by illness or want to take a trip, and to make their homes available if divorce or death leaves the children alone. The parents may be uncertain about how much help they can provide, or should provide, but not about their continued commitment to their children.

Children who live nearby are likely to visit frequently; they may have keys to the parents' homes and treat the parents' homes as extensions of their own. Children who live farther away are likely to visit once or twice a year. If there is a summer place, a tradition may develop of the retirees, their children, and their grandchildren living there together for a week or a month. When they do not live close enough to see each other regularly, retirees and their children stay in touch by telephone.

Children make retirees' lives richer simply by their existence. The retirees' lives are enriched by knowing that the children are doing well, by seeing them, and by talking with them. Children who can do so will join the parents for family holidays.

Families tend to be socialistic: from each according to his resources, to each according to his needs. Several respondents had accepted continuing responsibility for grown children. A few, despite their retirement, continued to contribute to their children's tuition at medical or law schools or advanced their children money toward a down payment on a home or a home reconstruction project. Children in their twenties or thirties who came home after losing a job or a marriage might be supported for a time. Mr. Trexler, the former technician, said:

My son said that things weren't working in his marriage and would we be willing to take him home, for as long as it took to get back. And I said sure, because we love the kid. I mean he's a good boy, and we said there'd be no problems whatsoever. And that's the way it was. There was no thought about it. It was just yes, of course, because we always said to our children, once they left the place, please don't come back unless there's something radically wrong, but the door is always open.

Still, when children returned to their retired parents' home after a marital separation, perhaps bringing with them their own children from the marriage, the parents might well have mixed feelings. Mr. Ulrich and his wife argued about permitting their daughter, who had separated from her husband, to come with their six-year-old grandson for an indefinite stay. Mr. Ulrich saw nothing wrong in it; his wife said that their daughter would fall into a comfortable dependency, which she, for one, was unwilling to indulge. The daughter moved in but the issue remained unresolved.

A few respondents reported rifts with one or more of their children. Mr. Hindes, whose children had opposed his remarriage, concluded that the children were indifferent to his happiness. He continued to visit his children and grandchildren, but said that his own life was now distant from theirs. Several respondents reported only infrequent contact with a grown child whose life had taken a course they did not understand or did not sympathize with.

In a few instances grown children seemed to become overly solicitous after a retirement. One risk for retirees who are divorced or widowed is that their children will interpret their retirement as a demonstration that the retirees are in decline. Since the retiree lives alone, the children, in a role reversal, may treat the retiree as in need of care and attention.

This is not to say that retirees are not pleased when their children display concern. They recognize that eventually they may be dependent on them. But they do not want the children to hurry things. So long as the retirees are able to look after themselves, they would prefer it if the children lived their own lives and respected the retirees' ability to live theirs.

Mrs. Walker had supported herself and her children for years after her husband's early death. She had had to ask a solicitous daughter to recognize that she remained able to look after herself.

My daughter calls all the time. "Mom, what are you going to do? Come over." She's trying to take care of me—this reversal situation. I had a little conversation with her one day. She said, "Mom, Norm," her husband, "Norm will come and pick you up." They live about twenty-two miles south of here. Now I don't drive in the city and I like to be home before dark. So my daughter keeps saying, "Mom, Norm'll come and take you and bring you home." I said, "Susie, you're not helping me." I said, "You're taking away my confidence, Honey." I said, "I know what you mean, and I know it's with love, but please don't do that to me." I said, "If I want you to come, I'll ask. And if I say I have to leave at three o'clock, because it's going to be dark at four, don't ask me to stay until three-thirty, because I start getting upset."

She said, "Okay, Mom." She was almost a little apologetic. I said, "You don't have to be apologetic." I said, "That's what happens. And I know you're motivated by love and caring and wanting to take care of me. But that's what you do. And it's negative. It's not positive."

Mrs. Walker did ask her children for help when there were home maintenance tasks beyond her strength. What was important for her was not doing everything herself but remaining in control.

I do call on my children if I have to have physical things, like hanging up the curtains; I'll call them and ask them. I mean, I'm not a martyr. They can do that for their mother. Their mother does things for them. It works both ways.

It may be a part of the aging process that family leadership shifts to the younger generation and that the children assume increased familial responsibility. The children are now the ones who work and are out in the world. The children may begin to provide advice on investments and host the family holiday get-togethers. Parents are generally pleased by this development: they want to be able to turn to their children for assistance. But they want this development to occur on their schedule, not the children's, and generally they would prefer that it not happen immediately.

Tension between the generations can stem from the retirement of the one, the movement into full adulthood of the other. One respondent said that a married son had signed a purchase agreement for a home in the belief that he could count on the respondent for the down payment. The respondent was furious. He had no objection to helping but he wanted to be asked first. Yes, he was retired, but that did not mean that he had relinquished his place in the family; he, and not his son, would decide how he used his money.

As retirees look back on their lives within their firms and within their families, it can be the life at home that is seen to have been of greater importance. If the work had been all-absorbing at the time, it can seem from this retirement perspective as having cost more than they had realized by keeping them from closer relationships with their children and from greater participation in their children's development.

Most of our respondents believed that their children provided the ultimate meaning of their lives. When they looked back over their careers, they felt that their work alone had been insufficient to justify their having lived. Someone else could have done what they had done—and would the world really be the poorer if the work had not been done at all? Many felt that it was because they had had their children, had raised them and launched them, that their lives had meaning.

Some retirees, perhaps especially men, cherish the idea of their children carrying part of themselves into the future. Mr. Crittenden, mulling over what he had done in life, said:

What's the point of living? Not to work for the company, that's for sure. There's only one point, only one possible thing: not to improve the human race through your children, but to have children, because that is a type of immortality.'

Maybe it's tied up with this idea of immortality. Couple of weeks ago [at the beach] I saw my son get my granddaughter and rig up a sunfish and take off. I thought, geez, when did I teach him how to sail? And then it sort of came and it brought back some happy memories. Some of these happy memories might be tied to that—that it's not only your genes but some of your skills that you've taught. Maybe there is some immortality.

Mr. Crittenden was also pleased that his sons would carry his family name into the future.

I was very careful to get a picture of me, my son, and my grandson. I have three male generations right there. And that picture means something to me. There's my name. And three males. It isn't as though you don't love your granddaughter and so forth, but I think this is tied in, in some way, about trying to rationalize some way to be immortal, even if it's only a name.

Most among our retirees who were parents were pleased simply to be parents. And they could feel, at least to an extent, some fulfillment of their own lives if their children were doing well enough, had good jobs, satisfactory marriages, and a secure place in the community. And grandchildren provided still further reassurance.

Grandchildren

Grandchildren strengthen retirees' sense of familial continuity. Perhaps even more than with one's own children, there can be an awareness with grandchildren that they are emissaries to the future. Retirees sometimes want to do what they can to equip them with strengthening memories. Dr. Cooper, a former university scientist, spoke about his responses to his first grandchild.

The first time I saw my first grandchild—that's now three and a half years ago; he's the son of my older daughter—I was overwhelmed by a feeling that this kid didn't ask to come into this world and that we had a terrible responsibility therefore. We called him here. It's our fault that he's here—hence our responsibility.

I didn't have that feeling with the birth of my own. I just didn't have it, although of course I felt responsible for them. But here it was very vivid and explicit that now I had to lead an especially good life, or something of that sort. When he gets big, I want him to remember me and basically to think that he's glad that I was his grandfather.

I can easily understand why I didn't have that feeling with my kids. I was young. In those days I was looking forward all the time. Now it's clear that death is something that's going to come. And now I think of my grandson, say at age twenty, and very likely I'll be dead by then—maybe not, but it's a significant probability—and it became important to me that he remember me well, that he be proud of me, that he be glad that I was his grandfather.

Retirement makes available the time to be with the grandchildren: to visit them or have them visit, and to join the parents in looking after them. Sometimes, when the children live nearby, the families of the retired become three-generation families spread over two households. And yet here, just as with part-time work, the retired want to protect their freedom. They are devoted to their grandchildren and they want to be with them regularly, but they also want to be able to do other things.

Mrs. Caldwell expressed this mixed view of grandparenting: desire to help her children by looking after their children, desire to be with her grandchildren, and reluctance to take on too much of a chore. She said:

My youngest son is married now, and they're expecting their first child. And like any young couple, you need two incomes. I mean, they bought a house. She's wonderful, a lovely girl. So she's going to work part time. It'll be Friday and Saturday. And my son will take care of the baby on Saturday, and I offered to take care of the baby on Friday. And they think that is wonderful, and I think that is wonderful. I mean, I am looking forward to it. I just love children. I love babies. And I just think it will be a nice thing for them and for me.

I wouldn't do it all the time. Like I told them, I said, "You know, I will not take care of a child seven days a week. No way." But if they need helping out or if they want to go out or if they want to go on vacation, I think it will be wonderful.

There is potential for friction here. The children of the retired can see their parents' free time as a family resource. Should they be stuck for babysitting, they can always call grandpa or grandma. The retired parents, on their part, can feel that being pressed into service without prior notice is an imposition. The grandchildren are loved, yes, but now the grandparents' plans have to be changed. And yet, at the same time, the grandparents can feel good about still being counted on. Mr. Trexler was typical of respondents with regular responsibility for grandchildren:

Yesterday I picked up my granddaughter over at her school a little after two. And my daughter, who's a nurse, comes home around four-thirty. She's working two days a week. She drops my granddaughter off at the school, and I take care of her after, until four-thirty. I wait until she comes home from the hospital. We play Yahtzee; we play different games. So that's what I do for two days of my week.

About a year and a half ago she started preschool, and then we took care of her for a couple of hours a couple days a week. But not a steady diet of five days. I don't know how people can do that. It's an awful job, because it's like bringing up another family again.

But everything worked out good. And I go over there twice a week, and she and I get along fine. No problems whatsoever. We never have any fights or arguments. And it's just marvelous.

Mr. Trexler found a satisfactory compromise between looking after his granddaughter and retaining his ability to use his time as he wished. Five days a week would have been an awful job, but two days a week was just marvelous. Two days a week did not mean being required once again to have continuing responsibility for child care, but it neverthe-less permitted the development of a relationship that was gratifying to the grandparent and, one may presume, to the grandchild as well.

Parents

Retirees' parents who remain alive are usually in their eighties and nineties. Many of them are infirm. A few respondents described retirements in which much of their energy was given to looking after an aging parent. Mrs. Pierce, the former marketing manager, had had some training as a nurse and was dismayed by the treatment her mother was receiving in a nursing home. Once she herself felt well enough to help, she began staying with her mother through much of the day. Another respondent, Mrs. Ellery, who retired by giving her construction company to her son, also gave much of her time in retirement to helping her mother. To be able to do that had been among her reasons for retiring.

In retirement, another thing I looked forward to was being able to help my mother, who is eighty-eight years old. I could not help her as much as I wanted to because the job I was doing was a full-time job every day of the week, weekends included. I was always available, that being part of my business strategy. There was nobody really to take over when I answered the phone except the machine, and I had a very strong feeling that I should always answer it. So I wanted to have some free time to go whenever I wanted down to see my mother to take care of her.

As it turned out, this summer she was moved into a very, very fine continuing-care home. And suddenly we had to spend three weeks clearing out her home, selling everything, and so on. And I could do that, whereas before I could not have done that.

Retirees regularly stayed in touch, often daily, with aged parents who lived within driving distance. Mrs. Aubrey, a town official before her retirement, would not travel with her retired husband because she wanted to continue her daily visits with her mother, who was in a nursing home. Retirees whose parents lived at a distance might rely on a sibling to look after them, but often experienced guilt that they themselves were not doing more.

In no case in our sample was a parent or parent-in-law taken into a retiree's home, although a couple of respondents spoke of parents being cared for in siblings' homes. Respondents seemed rather to support aged parents in the parents' homes or in nursing homes. When their parents continued to live independently, respondents looked in on the parents regularly, helped them with bills, and helped them obtain in-home help. When the parents could not care for themselves, respondents helped them find residences in which they would obtain assistance.[9]

Reverend Winsett, retired from a ministerial post, displayed both the continuing responsibility of retirees for aged parents and the ways in which they typically helped:

We have the major concern of my wife's mother. My mother-in-law's in her nineties; she's up and around but needs a lot more care. Her health is poor. She has crippling arthritis. She doesn't always get dressed. Her memory is failing, although her mind is still sharp. And her finances have run out. So we're in the process of determining nursing home or what for her. It's been a concern. The long-term-care people have come to visit her, and she's waiting to hear from the doctor again, and then a final decision as to whether she qualifies for nursing home or not.

My wife takes care of her finances, her Social Security, and her SSI. My wife writes the checks and juggles the funds to pay this one or pay that one, if possible. Her mother is house poor. She's gone through all her money. They cannot shut off her gas and her lights, so we just let those mount up and then eventually when she dies we'll sell some of her possessions and pay those things off. And we're willing to contribute if we have to, but at this point it's not been necessary. We do have an older couple in their sixties who are staying there in exchange for room and board. We were paying them, but we're not able to pay them anymore.

My wife and I go over just about every day to visit her for a half an hour or an hour or so. That's part of our routine. Occasionally we take her out for a ride, take her to the hairdresser. She can do that. Or we'll have her at our home for a meal.

My brother-in-law'd been in the Army for twenty years and retired. He's not working at all, hasn't worked for several years. He's just turned sixty-two. We're hoping they'll stay through the winter. It would make things easier for us. They have her at their home every Sunday for dinner. And my brother-in-law and I usually pick up the rubbish every week.

Retirees sometimes view parents' experience as indicators of what may lie ahead for them. They may resolve not to become residents of a nursing home themselves, or resolve to enter only a very good one. They may also resolve not to be a burden to their own children—to look after themselves, one way or another, until they die. Mr. Critten-den said, "I think one of the biggest gifts you can give to your children is not dollars in an estate, but the fact you were able to take care of yourself, or have someone take care of you, rather than imposing on their lives."

Retirees' relationships with their parents, as with their children, are lifelong. In each case identification, obligation, and love are inter-twined. At the same time there is likely to be belief that the indepen-dence of all should be protected.

Chapter Eight

A Good Retirement

One of our respondents, Mr. Gilbert, retired from running a business installing and repairing business equipment. He believed his retirement had significantly improved the quality of his life. It did so not by relieving him of work he found unappealing—all in all he had liked his work—but rather by making it possible for him to enrich his life with new activities.

Mr. Gilbert's retirement appeared to us to be successful in the sense that Mr. Gilbert felt realized and engaged and yet remained in control of his time. His account may suggest how one kind of good retirement, a retirement based on a core commitment, can be fashioned.

To be sure, Mr. Gilbert was unusually able to shape his retirement. As the majority owner of a successful small business, he had total freedom to decide when he would retire. He was in excellent health. His finances were good enough for him to have made a substantial donation to the college from which he graduated, and he was confident that he and his wife had enough money for the rest of their lives. He and his wife enjoyed each other's company. And he knew what he wanted to do with the time he would have when he no longer worked. But nothing in Mr. Gilbert's management of his retirement is in principle out of other people's reach.

Mr. Gilbert had begun to think seriously about retirement at age fifty-five.

Five years before I was sixty, I started a slow formulating of what I would like to do and how I would like to do it. And I said, "Gee, I think I'd like to work with wood and make furniture when I retire." And I set a benchmark, sixty, and then I'm going to school and I'm going to make furniture.

It didn't come as a sudden inspiration. I was always in love with woodworking. I always did something with wood—never anything on the order of making furniture, but I could pass for a carpenter.

I'm an engineer by training and when I was in college they had what they called Summer Shop, where you went through all the steps of making a wooden pattern for castings, then worked in the foundry. Working in the woodworking shop, I really enjoyed that. It always stayed with me from then on, that I enjoyed working with wood.

One end of our living room had an old-fashioned fireplace, and there were two windows there. My wife says, "It's pretty old-fashioned, windows and all that; what can we do about it?" So I tore all that out and rebuilt it and paneled it and built a new mantle piece. It was pleasurable. I guess it was I was doing something creative. And it enhanced the appearance of the room.

If you have a little bit of nerve, you tackle something, knowing that if you get into trouble you can go out and find yourself a carpenter to save you. I put in a playroom for the children in the basement of the house. I wouldn't tackle something that was over my head. And I never did anything major because my career took up a lot of time, including traveling a lot.

Mr. Gilbert retired because he wanted to do something new. He was also ready to stop working, but that was not his primary reason for retiring.

I didn't miss getting out of the business, really, because I had this game plan. I knew what I was going to do and I was eighty percent sure I'd enjoy it. So it was not leaving and saying, "Now what am I going to do? What will I do with my time?"

While I was working, it was enjoyable and it was productive and I was doing what I could do reasonably well. But after you do it for forty years, you get a little bit tired of the same thing. But it wasn't like I had to get away from it. Not at all. I enjoyed what I was doing. Even when it was tough, it was still something that I didn't dread getting up in the morning for.

Mr. Gilbert had earlier given the men who worked for him a

minority stake in his firm: 49 percent of its stock. Then, a year before his planned date of retirement, he stepped down as the firm's chief executive.

I knew who was going to take over the business, so about a year before I was going to retire I told all these people that I'm not going to work forever, and I made Marty president of the company.

Mr. Gilbert was surprised by the change in the way he was treated by his former employees once he stopped being the boss. They may have liked him as much as ever, but he now mattered less. Mr. Gilbert seemed to take the change in stride.

We used to have monthly meetings. Well, when you hold a meeting and you're the boss, everybody laughs at your bad jokes. Now I'm sitting at the foot of the table and Marty's at the head of the table. Nobody's looking at me anymore. Nobody's laughing at my bum jokes. They're laughing at *his* bum jokes.

I realized at that first meeting that, wow, now I don't sign their checks, they don't pay that much attention to me. Even though these men had been with me for years—at that point one had been with me twenty-five years—Marty had taken my place. They were looking to him as the boss, the guy they had to contend with.

I never thought about it, but they were paying homage to me because I was the guy that was signing the checks. I wasn't the charmer I thought I was. And it was kind of a shock to suddenly find that because I'm not sign-ing their checks anymore, I'm not the sage, the guy with all the answers. It's a strange sensation, a little startling, a little disquieting, but not traumatic. I didn't lose sleep over it, because I recognized what was going on.

As he approached his retirement date, Mr. Gilbert had to work out how he would dispose of his 51 percent ownership of the business. He decided, finally, to sell it to his former employees for the business's available cash.

I had nine men working for me for a long time, twenty-odd years. About ten years prior to my retirement I gave 49 percent of the business to them. Then when I was going to retire, I sold them my 51 percent for the cash in the bank. I sold the used desks and the used computers and the used office equipment for what they were worth. One guy put his hand up and said, "I'll buy them," and I said, "You got them."

Mr. Gilbert did not ask his former employees to pay anything for the business's reputation or relationships with clients or current contracts. Although Mr. Gilbert denied it, the sale expressed a continued concern for his former employees. It acknowledged that Mr. Gilbert and the employees were related by bonds of affection as well as employment. But only business concerns figured in Mr. Gilbert's explanation for giving his stake in the business to its ongoing staff.

I gave the business away because if you're going to sell a service business such as mine, you're selling personalities. If I sold it to somebody else, a group of them could have quit and gone across the street and gone into business themselves. And if I offered it to them for sale at, let's say, five times earnings, and they said, "No," what was I going to do? Also, let's say they agreed to buy it for a substantial price. Then they'd be struggling for the next five years to pay me off. And let's say one year business got bad, what would happen? I'd run back to protect my money. I didn't want to do that. So I said, "I'll take whatever there is in the bank; you can have the business."

Mr. Gilbert's display of continued regard for his former employees was matched by them. Mr. Gilbert was welcomed to the business's board of directors and also to its yearly Christmas party. In his account Mr. Gilbert minimized the meanings of these invitations, but it seems likely that he was pleased by them.

I'm on the board of directors but I think they have to do that, corporate-wise. They have a meeting, I think it's twice a year now, and I give them a little bit of advice. I don't know if they take it, but I give it to them anyway. And I go to the Christmas party once a year.

Mr. Gilbert also functioned as an unofficial adviser to the new head of his former business.

I meet with Marty once in a while to give him a little advice or just to hold his hand a little. It's his initiative. I have no financial interest. But it's always flattering to be called on for advice. I had been in the business for forty-odd years and there are certain nuances in the business. Marty's a very capable guy, but you have to experience it.

For example, he called me and said, "Let's have breakfast; I got some things I want to discuss." I talked with him about how business is off. And I said, "You got to let two people go." "Oh, I hate to do that." I say, "I hated to do it too, but either do that or give up your salary. Which do you want to do?" He said, "Well, I'm not going to take a cut in salary." I say, "Well, you got to fire two people. You don't have enough business to carry them." He knew that, but he just had to have someone to lean on that could say, "You got to fire them."

By acting as a consultant to his replacement, Mr. Gilbert briefly returned to the identity of businessman and engineer that he had maintained throughout his career. Yet he was in the process of relinquishing it; he had little regret when a visit to a trade show demonstrated that he no longer was current in his former field.

I've lost a lot of touch with what's going on; the industry is changing at such a rapid pace. I went to a trade show and didn't even recognize the equipment. I knew a few people, but I said, "What am I doing here? I'm a stranger to this. I really don't belong." And that was the end of that.

When Mr. Gilbert first decided to do woodworking, he applied to a school highly regarded for instruction in crafts. He was at first rejected, but applied again and was then accepted.

About a year and a half before I retired, I applied to a woodworking program. And they turned me down. I kept on their case and they finally said, "Well, we'll take you, but there's an eighteen-month waiting list." So I said, "Terrific, that will fall right on schedule." Then they called me and said: Could I start a month early? I said, "Absolutely," because I had already turned the business over to Marty. I retired and the next day started going to school.

Mr. Gilbert was almost immediately comfortable at the school. He was accepted there by people who shared his interests. Mr. Gilbert began to revise his sense of what he was about.

It turned out to be fun, going back to school. It's an interesting school. It's a trade school, one of the best trade schools in the United States. I had thought that I would be the old poop among a bunch of kids out of vocational school. It turned out not so. The school attracts older people. I think the average age when I was there was thirty-seven. I was admittedly the oldest, but the next down was about a year younger than me, fifty-nine.

The people that I was involved with, the one just younger than me was a mechanical engineer who had his own business. There was a professional skater who decided you can't make a living that way; there were two retired Army officers; there were a couple of arts majors. There were a couple of kids from vocational school. There were a couple of carpenters. It was a wonderful mix of people and it was a great two years. I couldn't wait to go to school in the morning. When there were days off for some holiday, I used to go anyways.

A short time after completing the crafts program Mr. Gilbert rented space in a building of workshops. There he was able to share tools and space with other furniture makers. The other furniture makers had lifestyles different from Mr. Gilbert's, but they endorsed Mr. Gilbert's commitments and supported his efforts.

I rent space in this shop. It's three big rooms. There are six furniture makers like myself in the shop. Each one works for himself. I just share the power tools—all the hand tools are mine. The center room is where the row of machinery is, and then in my room there are three furniture makers and then another room with three makers. They're young people. The things that they think are fun and their lifestyle, we're really in another world.

On my floor there's someone who does restoration of antiques. He's a super craftsman in that area. I have a job coming up that I'm bidding on; I just didn't know how to do it, so I went over to see him and I said, "How would you do this?" He gave me a couple of suggestions, because he's been at it all his life.

I feel free to ask anybody for an opinion. They'd probably say that I'm stodgy, but I think they would say that my work is good. It's not as good as this fellow's—his joinery is superb—but it's as good as anybody else's in the shop. And there's a certain amount of professionalism. They wouldn't criticize my work because they wouldn't think it would be right to do it, because we're in the same shop.

I work about thirty hours a week, approximately eight to two-thirty. Three o'clock, I'm tired physically, because I'm dragging lumber around. As you build something, every time you add a stick to it, it gets heavier. And you add another stick, and it gets heavier. And you add some more, and it gets heavier. And then you got to move it. So you say, "Somebody help me move this thing." Or if I need help to hold onto something, I can ask somebody to give me a hand, as I do for them.

Mr. Gilbert's estimated thirty hours of work a week were a lot of hours for work as a retirement activity. But Mr. Gilbert was not obligated to work that many hours. Only rarely would he commit himself to producing a piece by a particular date, and then only if the piece was easy to make. And when he and his wife wanted to take a couple of weeks away, he would just close his workshop and go.

Mr. Gilbert's finished products were admirable. He was becoming ever more skilled and so took on ever more challenging projects. His aims were aesthetic: to make something truly satisfying.

It's just a lot of rough boards, and suddenly you end up with something that's livable and that I think is handsome. My designs are tried and true. I don't generally go out on a toot and do something odd. It's something that's got some basis in furniture history. And just seeing it when it's done and looking at it and admiring it myself—if a piece doesn't look right, I throw it away and start all over again. If something doesn't look right, I'm just not going to tolerate it because I have to satisfy me and make myself happy about how it comes out.

I'm making more and more sophisticated stuff. I'm finishing a chest on a chest, which is pretty complex. And I'm starting an executive desk. So it's challenging. I never make the same piece twice, so everything is a brand new set of problems. And fortunately they've come out well so far.

Mr. Gilbert sold most of his products, but his work was not important to him as a source of income. Although he was gratified that the products were salable, what really mattered was the satisfaction he drew from having made them.

I've probably lost money on every piece I've made so far. I mean the rent, the light, the heat, the materials—I've lost money. I figured out how much I made on one piece, and I made about a dollar and a quarter an hour. I don't know how to charge. Some woman, she wants me to make a bench to go with her piano. I would like to make that because it's a very ornate piano. So I figured twelve hundred or thirteen hundred dollars, and I mentioned it to this fellow who does restoration, and he said, "You got to get three thousand dollars for that." Do I have the nerve to ask that? Well, I'll try her on for size and see what happens.

Hand making furniture is a very slow, laborious process. And very expensive, because I'm cutting one stick at a time, then I have to remeasure, reset the machine, then I cut another stick. If you're making a hundred piano benches, well, you set the machine and you cut a hundred pieces of wood, you set it again and you cut another hundred. Jam the stick in and it comes out finished. I don't have any of that.

When I start on a piece, as it progresses I say, "Gee, it would look good if I used a different kind of veneer on the back instead of straight veneer." So suddenly it costs me another five hundred bucks. But I want to do it because it will look better. I made a bed for someone and it's Empire style. And I started on that and I saw a picture of one in an old book that had swans carved on the front. I wanted to do some carving; I hadn't done any serious carving. I said, "Would you like swans?" So she said, "Oh, I'd love it." So I said, "Okay, two hundred fifty dollars a swan." And it must have cost me five or six hundred for a swan, because I never carved. It took me weeks to do it. But it came out very nicely.

In addition to undercharging clients, Mr. Gilbert sometimes gave pieces to family members as gifts.

In between jobs I'll make something for the family. One of those beds I made for my son, because I wanted him to have something of mine. And my daughter got married this past summer; I made a bed for her, as a wedding gift. So that takes me two months to make and that's zero income. It just costs me money for material and so on.

Mr. Gilbert did want to be paid for his work because that would demonstrate that the pieces had worth and that his was a serious enterprise rather than self-indulgence. He had worked for no pay and had not liked it: just after completing his course in the crafts school he had served as an unpaid instructor in a local high school. He said that as a volunteer he had not really mattered.

After I finished school someone asked me if I would help them teach at a high school. They have a woodworking shop and I knew the man who ran it. So I'd go there two mornings a week and help him teach the boys. And it just was I was not part of the team. If they had said, "We'll give you five dollars an hour," and then they'd come around to find out if I was earning my five bucks an hour, I think that would have meant something. But I was just kind of the guy who comes in and goes about his little bit of help and then goes home and nobody cares if he doesn't show up. I wouldn't do that again. If they wanted me, they would have to show they wanted me by paying me something. Then you've got a responsibility. I guess we all want responsibility.

Mr. Gilbert's woodworking did bring with it responsibility. When Mr. Gilbert accepted an order from a client, he was obligated to fulfill it. He liked having orders because that gave him a reason to do the work. Payment gave closure to the project.

If you said you wanted a dresser made, for example, or a bed or a chair, well, I'd make it for you. I'd get an idea of what you wanted in terms of shape, size, you know. Show you pictures. I like to make pieces that are typically Federal period. That's about 1800 to 1850. Not everybody wants it, but I would steer you into something that's appropriate for your home. Give me a deposit and I go to work and make it, deliver it to you, and you pay me. Period, the end.

Mr. Gilbert's emotional investment in making furniture began changing him. The changes showed in his interests when not working and in his thoughts regarding the future.

I'm having a wonderful time. I still can't wait to get to work. I'm making what I want, and I'm doing something creative. Even though the design isn't mine, I have nuances that are mine. I don't copy something.

My entire perspective is now oriented around furniture. We took a trip to see a museum of American furniture. There was a chair that I knew was there, and they pulled it out of the warehouse for me and I took pictures of it.

Maybe I'll get tired of doing woodworking. I don't know. I don't see it yet.

There are a lot of things I haven't done yet that I want to try. You know, it's a craft, and you keep improving, and there are still things you haven't done yet.

For Mr. Gilbert, furniture making permitted expression of a long-held passion. It brought with it membership in a community of people whom Mr. Gilbert respected and with whom he shared goals and, to an extent, values. His work was admired and wanted by his friends and by still others who happened across something he had done. And it provided Mr. Gilbert with challenge and the opportunity to improve, all at his own pace. And with all this, Mr. Gilbert's work was free of the stresses he had experienced while maintaining an enterprise on which his income and the income of his employees depended. Plus, it gave Mr. Gilbert the freedom to decide for himself how he would use his time, how much time he would give to the work and on what schedule, and when he would take vacations and days off.

Mr. Gilbert's marriage was one in which there was a good deal of companionship even though he was in his workshop six hours a day. When we talked with his wife, she described their day as beginning with companionate activity.

We get up early, at six o'clock, take a shower, and go out for a walk. We walk a mile every morning regardless of the weather, unless it's snowing or a downpour. We take the dog and the two of us go out for about twenty-five minutes, then come home and eat breakfast, and he goes to work.

I make him walk. I won't walk alone early in the morning like that. I insist that he go with me. We're not sports people, so if we take a mile walk every morning, I feel at least we're getting our exercise. And it's nice in the early morning. It's good to get out in the air. We get a chance to talk to each other if we have a problem. We talk about everything, like when we were having problems with one of the children. Sometimes we don't even need to talk.

Mr. Gilbert said that his wife was entirely supportive of his retirement work.

You've been married for years, you know what your wife is thinking and she knows what you're thinking. She reads my mind; I read her mind. I know how she's going to respond to 90 percent of the situations. I know she knows how

I'm going to respond. I always wanted to make antique furniture, and my wife concurred. She said, "That's all right. Let's do it."

Mrs. Gilbert was not without some regrets that her husband was so involved in furniture making. It ruled out long vacations in a warm climate. There was a bit of wistfulness in her voice as she described the limitations her husband's retirement work imposed.

It's a whole new career. It's different entirely from what he was doing. But there wasn't really any difference, because he left his old job and went right into school immediately.

A lot of our friends are in Florida. If my husband wasn't happy and wasn't working, and he said to me, "Let's go," I'd go. But he has commitments now. When you're going to make something for somebody, you have to get it done. He did say he'd take, like, a week or so in the summer. And we had two weeks this winter. And maybe he can take two weeks in the summer, spread it apart or something.

Yet Mrs. Gilbert was proud of her husband's skills and supportive of his work. She said:

He was always good with wood. He makes antique furniture, and it comes out gorgeous. His work is very good. The school recommends him for things, so the school must think he's good.

The Gilberts seemed to have found an acceptable compromise of their different desires for the management of their retirement time: Mr. Gilbert closed his shop for a couple of weeks in the winter, and Mrs. Gilbert accepted that he did not want to be away any more than that. Both of the Gilberts supported the basic framework of their lives in retirement.

Conclusion

Part I: What's Been Learned

A good deal of ground has been covered in the previous chapters. Here are what I believe to be the most noteworthy observations and findings.

Retirement means changing how one relates to the social world. It means leaving a career, a community of work, and a way of life. It is likely to bring with it extraordinary freedom. It may also expose the retiree to social isolation.

By and large, the more orderly the retirement, the better. It is better if the retirement is long planned and coworkers are aware of the plans, and if it makes sense in terms of the retiree's career and the retiree's marriage. Because the retirement will affect the retiree's spouse as well as the retiree, retirement decisions are best made jointly.

Retirement ends the associations of work. The way in which the retiree and the people with whom the retiree worked will later think about the associations will be affected by the way in which they are ended. Those who have been pushed into retirement or for whom retirement was a kind of quitting are thereafter burdened by a sense of important relationships that ended badly. Their former coworkers, too, are likely to feel uncomfortable about the entire course of the association.

There seem to be fewer financial problems immediately after retirement than people anticipate. But retirees often feel some uncertainty about long-term financial stability. Their primary concern is that they may at some point have to pay for health care. And, indeed, need for a treatment or service not covered by Medicare or health insurance, such as long-term nursing care, can derail all but the best-funded retirements.

More of an immediate concern for many retirees is the impact on them of the loss of their community of work. Some degree of social isolation can be inescapable in the short run for retirees who have no other community membership with which to replace their membership in the community of work. Most manage initial social isolation reasonably well. Some, especially those who are unmarried, seem to have continuing difficulties. The conjunction of a recent marital loss and retirement can be devastating.

There are many forms of activity available to the retired, each with its own mix of contributions and constraints. Part-time work—two days a week is often proposed as ideal—can maintain linkage to an occupational community and still permit enough freedom for other things. Hobbies, if they are not entirely solitary, can provide the sense of flow, of immersion in an activity, that is otherwise lost with the ending of work. Voluntary activities provide engagement with others as well as opportunity to be of service while yet allowing control over one's time and efforts. Membership in organized programs can be valuable if it brings with it the potential for satisfactory interchange. Travel can be a wonderful, enriching break from the ordinary. Puttering can make for quietly enjoyable days.

Perhaps most important for the quality of life in retirement is the retiree's relationship with his or her life partner. As couples move toward retirement their marriages change from partnerships in the management of home and family to companionships. More time is likely to be spent together. Retirement then provides still more time together. Being able to enjoy that additional time together can decide whether the retirement will be gratifying or burdensome.

Part II: Advice to a Prospective Retiree

The experiences of retirees that have been reported in earlier chapters can be used to suggest what might make for a good retirement. Here is what I would say to someone anticipating a retirement within the next year or so. I will begin with money, but most of my attention will be given to other determinants of the quality of the retiree's life.

I should say that most of the respondents whose reports provide the basis for my advice retired from middle-class careers, and the advice I offer is primarily directed toward others who, like them, are retiring from middle-class careers.

Money

You probably would do well to consult a financial adviser whom you can trust to work out the best way of estimating your retirement needs and managing your retirement finances. Based on the reports of our respondents, however, my guess is that if you own a home outright, without a mortgage, and can count on an income that is at least half your highest salary, you can manage all right for the first years of retirement. Expenses for ongoing life drop in retirement, and the larger expenses of earlier life—children's college tuition, especially—will likely be absent.

After the first years inflation can pose a problem. But most people, if they have to, can reduce their standard of living without experiencing great harm. What is essential is that even with inflation you and your spouse have enough money over the course of your lives to protect your independence: to cover food, clothing, shelter and the taxes and utility bills that accompany shelter, the telephone and e-mail that link you to others, and the health care that is likely to be needed.

Retiring with enough in savings and investments—including your home—to compensate for any loss in the value of the dollar would be desirable. Investment advice is not something I am competent to give, but I would suggest checking out U.S. Treasury inflation-protected securities as a way of maintaining the present value of some of your savings.

Automobiles are expensive and you might think of ending dependence on them. How you do that will depend on where you live and whether you can call on alternative services such as public transportation, relatively inexpensive car rental, or transportation services for seniors. On the other hand, your aim should be to maximize the quality of your life; if driving is important for that, and you have to cut expenses, you might try cutting elsewhere.

The most serious threat to your financial stability comes from health care costs. The few respondents in our study who had serious financial problems in the first years of their retirement foundered because of the costs of health care. If your firm's retirement program permits you to choose among health care options, go for the best health insurance you can get. If you will be without health insurance when you retire, get disinterested advice. Medicare may be all you need, but check.

If your retirement date is flexible, before you take the plunge look into the health care coverage of those for whom you feel responsible. If someone for whom you feel responsible is uninsured, your retirement savings could be eroded by that person's medical needs. Make sure your finances are adequate to the challenge.

Planning your retirement

Think through the emotional importance of work for you. How do you now feel on weekends? On vacations, were you ready to get back to the job before the vacation ended? If your answers to these questions suggest that work is emotionally important for you, retirement without work may not be what you want. Chances are, you already have some foreboding about retirement. If you can, you might want to postpone it. You surely should accept part-time postretirement work if that option is available to you. If you have to retire and no part-time work is a possibility in your firm, you might want to start looking into what might be available elsewhere. Generally it is easier to find full-time work than part-time, but you might want to be ready to accept either.

Many retirees for whom work is important prefer part-time to full-time work because part-time work provides much of a full-time job's responsibility, community, and opportunity for achievement while permitting an adequate measure of the freedom that is retirement's gift. Part-time work can also have the great merit of limiting the kind of responsibility that brings about stress. The best kind of retirement work is engaging yet stress free and permissive of lots of time off.

Many retirees find that the amount of work that works best is around sixteen hours a week, plus or minus a few hours. But some retirees have been able to gain the benefits of working by serving as consultants and showing up only once a month; others have been able to realize a reasonable amount of retirement's freedom while working as much as three days a week.

If work is essential to your emotional economy and you are nevertheless headed for retirement, and neither full-time nor part-time work is available to you, consider volunteering. It will be important to find a position in an enterprise whose services or products you respect. Try to find a job that utilizes your occupational skills and experience and that brings with it genuine responsibility. A retired executive might, for example, look into the Service Corps of Retired Executives (SCORE), a national volunteer organization that makes former executives available as advisers to people who are just starting a business. Volunteering is not the same as paid employment, but the closer your volunteer position comes to being a real job, the better. And volunteering is superior to paid employment in that it is easier to take time off from it.

If work is not essential to your emotional economy—and for many retirees it is not—you are in the fortunate position of being able to decide the mix of retirement activities that will best suit you without worrying about how to fit other activities around part-time work. Although you now have all the freedom in the world to do whatever you want to do—paint or write a novel or travel or anything else—if you are entirely confident of your plans, you should do as much arranging as you can as soon as possible. Setting things up often takes time. It seems useful to begin the transition to retirement earlier rather than later.

If you are not sure what you will do in retirement, except for vague plans to get your papers in order or to do a bit of traveling or to take it easy for a while, begin thinking more specifically about your life in retirement. To the extent you can, explore possible activities. At the same time, keep in mind that what seems to be attractive now may be less so as you become more familiar with it. This is especially the case with volunteering. If you have been a volunteer during your working life, you know what to expect, but if you have not, do not make firm commitments until you have tried it. The same goes for hobbies—unless you have practiced a hobby for a while and know it is right for you, wait until actual retirement before you redo the sun porch as a studio. Also, keep in mind that people and their needs often change after retirement. A hobby that offers relaxation when you are working may be boring when work no longer stresses you out. So do as much early exploration as you can, but wait until your actual retirement before you commit yourself.

Leaving work

The terms on which you leave your work will affect your memories of your years on the job. Try to leave on as good terms as is possible. The more orderly your retirement, the better. Once you set your retirement date, let the people with whom you work know. Telling them that you will retire will change your role in the work group because your coworkers will start preparing for your absence. But that is as it should be.

After you have left the firm, your former coworkers are unlikely to remain part of your social world. One or two may, but you will have to find a basis for continued association with them other than events at work. Still, unless you move your residence, chances are that you will bump into former coworkers now and again. At such times it will be nice to experience genuinely warm feelings rather than uneasy embarrassment. Leaving on good terms makes this possible. And this is not only a matter of having your former coworkers think well of you; your sense of how they feel about you will affect your feelings about yourself.

Less orderly retirements, in which people have retired precipitously to escape a disliked situation, or have been pushed into retirement by superiors or colleagues, make for unhappy transitions to retirement. Retirees' experience in retirement can still be good, but their memories of their time at work are likely to be tarnished. If this happens, it happens; but try to avoid it.

Have a plan for your last days at work. Decide when you will move your personal files out of the workplace and which of your possessions you will take home. Decide, also, how much effort you will give to preparing your office and your projects for your successor. Before you leave the firm for the last time, say good-bye to everyone you have worked with.

If someone proposes having a retirement lunch or party for you, accept the proposal. People contemplating retirement sometimes decide they will refuse a retirement party for various reasons—they have mixed feelings about the workplace, or they hope to retain an affiliation and do not want coworkers to shrug them off as retired, or they love their work so much that retirement is painful. Or they may believe that retirement parties and retirement lunches are boring events at which coworkers are required to say things they do not really mean. Despite these reasons for declining formal recognition of your retirement, accept it. Later, looking back, it will help you feel good about having been a member of the work group. Our interviews suggest that even a bittersweet retirement event is better than no event.

Try to leave the firm on good terms with everyone, including those who acted as if the firm would be the better for your departure. On the other hand, if your retirement was imposed on you, if you were pushed out in a hostile maneuver, you may later be more comfortable with yourself if you stand up for yourself. If you have been genuinely mistreated, it may be a good idea to talk with a lawyer who knows something about the laws against age discrimination. Even if there is nothing you can do, or nothing you want to do, learning your legal rights may make you feel better about yourself. If so, it is likely to be worth the cost. Furthermore, a good legal representative can sometimes negotiate terms of severance that are better than those you could obtain yourself.

Moving

Sometimes people plan to move when they retire. They want to escape the winter snows or to be closer to their children and grandchildren or to live as an expatriate in an attractive, low-cost foreign country. Moving for these reasons can be chancy from the standpoint of quality of life. It is hard in retirement to make new friends with whom you can have the social life you probably have now. If you move to an area that is attractive to retirees, you will undoubtedly find people with whom to go to dinner, but it will be much harder to find people whom you feel as comfortable with as you do with your present friends—and even harder to find people you can call on in a pinch. Also, new places may not have the resources you have become used to: the doctor you have had for years, stores with which you are familiar, libraries, and colleges. You will have to get used to being an outsider to the natives who run things. If you are contemplating such a move, I recommend renting before buying, and spending a couple of weeks in the new region during each of two seasons.

The least chancy move may be from a house in the suburbs to a smaller place closer to the central city. Reasons for such a move might be that out in the suburbs you are dependent on an automobile or that your house is too big for you. Even then, I would be cautious about moving. I recommend talking with others who have made a similar move before undertaking it yourself.

Your marriage

Your retirement gives you a lot of time to be at home. Most couples, including those who are initially apprehensive about getting in each other's way, wind up pleased by the increase in their time together. Intrusiveness may well occur, but it usually turns out to be easily managed. It is an annoyance, but only a passing one, when one partner is on the phone when the other partner wants to use it, or one partner wants help with household accounting when the other partner is writing a letter. Accommodations to the other's presence are easily made, given good will and time. Also, in the absence of work's pressures and preoccupations, each partner is likely to be more flexible and more accessible.

Sometimes, though, husbands and wives are more comfortable with a certain amount of time alone. If your spouse is also retired or for another reason is not working, and the two of you need time alone, you may want to talk together about your joint routines. It may make sense for one of you to have activities that take him or her outside the home for much of the day. This is especially the case if you and your spouse have for some reason developed mixed feelings toward each other. Actually, if this is the case, it might be worth trying to improve the relationship. The quality of one's life in retirement is heavily affected by the quality of one's marriage.

In the not infrequent situation in which the husband retires while the wife remains at work, husbands tend to be ambivalent about acting as housekeepers. Some husbands who try to do the shopping and cooking and cleaning wind up disliking the social isolation and repetitive routine that are part of keeping house. To be sure, a couple of househusbands among our respondents developed a mix of in-the-house and out-of-the-house activities that together made for a satisfactory life. But a couple of others found part-time or full-time work to escape continuing as a househusband, and still others escaped being househusbands by packing their bags and going to Florida for the winter or spending the workweek right through the year in what had been the couple's summer home. In most cases men who had retired while their wives continued at work wanted their wives to join them in retirement.

To two-career couples in which the husband has retired first, I would recommend thinking through what is best for their continuing partnership as well as for each individually. Often the wife is younger than the husband or has only recently reached a position of scope and authority and is reluctant to leave work just yet. If it is possible for the husband to take on new work or, failing that, significant responsibility as a volunteer, that might be worth considering.

Retirement and kin

Living parents of retirees are usually in their eighties and nineties. If they are infirm, they can be a major responsibility. If you will be their primary caretaker because you are an only child or because your siblings live at a distance, attending to your parents' needs may absorb a fair amount of time and energy.

A widowed parent who lives alone is likely to be especially needful. Shopping, cooking, and cleaning can all be chores with which the parent will need help. A widowed parent who is in a residence for the aged, though needing less in the way of physical help, may nevertheless need the reassurance of a child regularly checking in to see that things are going well.

If there are siblings, have a conference with them to decide who will do what and how the costs of care will be met. If there is no insurance, or if insurance is inadequate, health-care costs can mount up. Even if there is insurance, special nursing can be expensive.

One of the attractions of retirement is that you can spend more time with your children and grandchildren. One of the problems of retirement is that your children may begin to view you as an on-call babysitter. Retirees tend to want regular contact with their children and grandchildren, and are happy sometimes to have responsibility for young grandchildren. But most feel, and some make explicit, that they are past their child-raising years and no longer want continuing responsibility for children.

If your children live nearby and have children of their own, you might want to arrange to look after the grandchildren a day a week or a couple of hours a day. You could have the children and grandchildren come for a few hours on the weekend or for supper on a weekend evening. You might be willing to have the grandchildren for a week or two while their parents go off on a child-free vacation. But you probably would not regularly want even as much as half-time responsibility for grandchildren.

Activities in retirement

There is no one way of organizing retirement that works for everyone. Just as people differ earlier in their lives in what constitutes for them a satisfactory life, they differ in retirement. There are, however, some principles worth keeping in mind.

Try for an optimal mix of engagement and freedom. For many retirees an optimal mix is one in which they have obligations for about half their time or slightly less. Retirees who have part-time work tend to find two days a week about right. Retirees who do not have part-time work might try for a combination of doing volunteer work, looking after grandchildren, and participating in organized activities. Obligating much more time than half the week can cost too much in freedom; obligating much less can foster a sense of marginality. But what is optimal for you may be different from what is optimal for others.

Choose activities that, in sum, replace the provisions of work that had been important to you. If an occupational identity mattered to you, try to find an activity, paid or voluntary, in which you will find support for that identity. For example, a former accountant might take on accounting responsibilities for a religious institution.

Try things you have always wanted to do but never got around to doing—but keep in mind that you might have had a good reason for not getting around to them. If you have always wanted to learn piano, take lessons. If the practicing and improving and the actual making of music work for you, great; if they do not, you have lost nothing. Most often the activities that will prove rewarding in retirement will be activities you pursued earlier in your life and already know to be gratifying—but do not limit yourself to these.

Include among your retirement activities something that helps you feel good about yourself. Most people need other people's recognition of their contributions or abilities or worth. Look for an activity that provides that. You might, for example, want to help in a church's food-distribution program. But again, if it is something you have not done before, it may turn out not to be what you want to do. With any activity you have not done before, maintain an exploratory outlook until you are sure that it will work for you.

Do not get down on yourself if you find that you like taking it easy. Chances are that you will have a better retirement if that is not all you do, but if it is a major part of what you do and you are happy with it, that is fine.

Some general comments might be made about the potential contributions of various activities.

Part-time work has much to recommend it. The income establishes that what you are doing has value to others. The job imposes a structure on your week, even if it requires only that you show up two or three afternoons. But make sure that it is relatively stress free and that it permits you the freedom to use your retirement time as you wish.

Not every occupation will provide opportunities for part-time work. Doctors and, to a lesser extent, lawyers and academics can usually find something if they look. Other professionals, and business people as well, may have a more difficult time finding part-time work in what have been their fields. If no appropriate part-time work is available, they might want to look into volunteering or teaching a course, perhaps in adult education.

The best volunteer activities are likely to be those that really matter, in which what you do makes a difference, and in which you already have a commitment of some sort to the group or institution for which you volunteer. It would also be good if the activities did not infringe too much on your freedom to do other things, nor impose stressful responsibility.

Hobbies are excellent if you really care about them. A recipe for a good hobby is that it involves you enough so that you are able to lose yourself in it, that it somehow connects you with other people, and that it gives you opportunity for recognition. If you are a reader, think about participating in a book club; if you are a photographer, have shows or teach classes in photography or join a camera club.

Joining an organized program like a folk-dance group or a language group can provide both an enjoyable experience and a community. Taking a class may or may not work in this way: participating actively is different from only occupying a seat and listening to a lecturer. If you participate actively, the class is, like other organized programs, a way of becoming engaged with others. If you only sit and listen, it is a kind of entertainment, a form of theater attendance. It will not connect you with others and can even increase your sense of marginality.

Many people plan to travel when they retire. They think of driving a recreational vehicle around the country or buying a rail pass in Europe or sailing the Caribbean. And, indeed, many find actual travel to be gratifying. The experience of traveling is dense with new people, new places, and new languages, customs, and foods. Traveling is a kind of expression of freedom, since you do not have to be any particular place or do any particular thing. But travel can also be wearing and uncomfortable and risky. If you are going to travel, choose not only the place you would like to visit but also the level of challenge you can manage. Reasonable advice might be to choose slightly less challenge than you think you can manage, because not everything will go right. If you have never traveled and are uncertain about your ability to deal with settings and arrangements you have never encountered, begin with a tour or a cruise.

Give time to your family, and especially to your spouse, children, and grandchildren. You are important to them, and they will carry your relationship with them forward into their own lives. And, as time goes on, your social circle may well constrict, in which case your relationships with them will become even more important to you.

There are things you will want to avoid in retirement. Illness, of course, is one, but that may not be within your control—although it is a good idea to maintain a healthy diet and an exercise program. Alcoholism, marital problems, and financial misadventure can all occur in retirement just as in earlier life, but now they might be harder to recover from: there is less time for righting oneself and going on. Retirement is not a good time of life to take risks with health, relationships, or finances.

You will want to savor the time that is entirely your own. But, as I have repeatedly noted, without engagement with others, life and self are diminished. A sense of purposelessness can invade the retirement, and depression can happen more easily.

Social isolation is likely to be a problem especially for those who had depended on their work to provide them with membership in a community. Retirement makes it easy to withdraw. Being needed by others—including parents and children and grandchildren—can be an antidote. A support group of some sort—a men's group or women's group, or participation in a senior center—can also be a good idea.

People can experience social isolation without knowing what is wrong. They know that they do not look forward to much of anything, and that they are restless when there is yet another evening with only television for company. They can step outside themselves and see that their lives are not what they want them to be. But they do not entirely recognize that the problem is social isolation. As for getting out and seeing people, they may feel that with their morale so low they would rather not.

Make sure that you do not fall into social isolation; it can feed on itself. Particularly at risk are those who live alone. If that is you, you might want to explore activities that link you to communities: programs for learning in retirement are one example; hiking clubs, if they are serious, are another. Find activities that you will enjoy, that you can involve yourself in, and that bring with them membership in a community. If something is available and you are not sure it will work, try it. There will be discomfort if you go once and not again, but if it works out you will find your life enriched.

A Meaningful Retirement

Retirement will happen to each of us, assuming only that death does not get to us first. Even if you are determined to work as long as you can, there will come a point at which your coworkers will want you to retire. Oliver Wendell Holmes, who remained a member of the Supreme Court into his nineties, was finally asked to retire by a delegation of colleagues. Assuming, again, that death does not make the issue moot, each of us will at some point have to make sense of a time in our lives in which not only is it no longer expected that we will work, it is expected that we will not.

One way of making sense of this removal from work is to regard it as a reward for a lifetime of labor. So we may be told, "You've worked long enough" and "You deserve a time for yourself." But there is a false note in these reassurances. I, at least, suspect that they are patronizing and that those who offer them actually believe that age has made us incapable and, as people who are incapable, no longer of social importance.

I prefer rather to insist that while retirement may mean that our energies or ambitions or zest for work are no longer up to the demands of the work we once did, this says nothing about our wisdom or concern for others or desire to continue to contribute to the social world. And even though we sacrifice some of the freedom of retirement by involving ourselves in the social world, I recommend a retirement in which we continue to care about others and work with them and for them, even if no longer in a paid position.

Keep time for yourself, yes, but not to the exclusion of continuing to play a role in the world. There is no reason in retirement to take on stressful commitments, but stress reduction does not require doing nothing. I know older people who have found serenity in Buddhist teachings who are also actively engaged in campaigns against smoking and in the politics of housing. If I were pressed to choose, I would choose contribution over serenity, but there is no inconsistency between them.

A part of making sense of later life is coming to terms with the fact that it is, indeed, later life. The critical choices of our lives—where we will be schooled and what will be our work and whom we will marry and how we will raise our children—all have been made and are irrevocable. We continue to have choices, but they are unlikely to be life changing. The choices we made earlier in our lives can be assessed and we are lucky if none of them are regretted, but we are now at an age where they must for the most part be accepted.

And yet the present and future are always open. There are always enterprises we can forward and people for whom we are important whose lives we can better. Even in retirement—*especially* in retirement—there is always something to do.

Acknowledgments

The study on which this book is based and the book itself have bene-
fited from the contributions of many people. I am grateful to them all.
Chief among contributors were, of course, the respondents. We asked
them to walk us through their experiences and they did it wonderfully
well.

The Institute of Aging, National Institutes of Health, provided the
research grant that made the study possible. Fellow members of
the project's core staff were Mary Coffey, Carolyn Bruse, and John
Drabik. Each was invaluable in dealing with the reams of interview
transcript. Joining me in interviewing were Ron Shachter, Lucille Rai-
mondo, Minnie Weiss, and, for the last round of interviewing, Harriet
Goodwin. Anna Marie Sant'Anna served as project director during a
year I was away at the Center for Advanced Study in the Behavioral
Sciences. We consulted on project management by phone, but she
made everything work.

From the very beginning of my work on the book, Jim O'Brien has
been a magnificent editor and sounding board. I am also grateful to
Jeff Burr, Frank Caro, and Sally Bould for knowledgeable reviews of
chapters, and to David Matz for an essential and acutely perceptive
response to an early draft of the book. Sarah Wernick, who is a book
doctor of extraordinary skill and intelligence, showed me how to organize chapter one. Frank Caro, as director of the Gerontology Institute of the University of Massachusetts, provided an indispensable

supportive setting for analysis and writing. Throughout the writing of the book, fellow members of the Friday Morning Men's Group offered encouragement as well as insightful responses to drafts of chapters.

When I entered the publishing phase of the project Sidney Kramer generously acted on my behalf in the management of contractual issues. Karen Bosc was a superb copy editor, identifying places where my argument needed attention as well as regularizing my more idiosyncratic sentence structures. Indeed, everyone at Cornell University Press has been extraordinarily good to work with. I want especially to thank Fran Benson, the editor in charge of the project. She repeatedly displayed judgment of a very high order. I am fortunate to have had her guidance.

As always, I am grateful to my wife, Joan Hill Weiss, for so very much. To say that this book could not have been written without her is to say the simple truth.

Notes

Introduction. What Does It Mean to Be Retired?

1. Dora L. Costa, *The Evolution of Retirement: An American Economic History, 1880–1990* (Chicago: University of Chicago Press, 1998).

2. For further discussion of the psychological definition of retirement and its relationship to other definitions, see Maximiliane E. Szinovacz and Stanley DeViney, "The Retiree Identity: Gender and Race Differences," *Journals of Gerontology, Psychological Sciences and Social Sciences* 54B, no. 4 (July 1999): 207–22.

3. R. S. Weiss, *Staying the Course: The Emotional and Social Lives of Men Who Have Done Well at Work* (New York: Free Press, 1990).

4. Things have changed since I wrote the book. But it seems to me that younger men in the professions and in executive and administrative positions have not so much reduced their ambitions at work as they have added the requirement that they share the tasks of homemaking and parenting.

5. In the section of acknowledgments at the end of the book I thank by name the other members of the Work and Family Research Unit of the University of Massachusetts. I am indebted to each of them.

6. My impression is that the volunteer women may have included two or three who were a bit more troubled by their retirement experience than most other women, but differences were not dramatic. The men from local institutions were not distinguishable from other executives and administrators in our sample.

7. The 1900 and 1950 statistics are from Costa, *The Evolution of Retirement*, 8. The year 2002 statistic is from the U.S. Bureau of Labor Statistics, "Civilian Labor Force Participation Rates by Sex, Age, Race, and Hispanic Origin, 1982, 1992, 2002, and Projected 2012," http://www.bls.gov/emp/emplab2002-03.htm.

8. U.S. Bureau of Labor Statistics, "Civilian Labor Force Participation Rates by Sex, Age, and Hispanic Origin, 1982, 1992, 2002, and Projected 2012," http://www. bls.gov/emp/emplab2002-03.htm.

9. U.S. Bureau of Labor Statistics, "Civilian Labor Force Participation Rates." In a presentation to Congress of findings from the University of Michigan's Health and Retirement Study, Robert Willis observed that "The downward shift in labor force par-

ticipation by the elderly that had begun in 1950 had started to slow and reverse itself by 1985." See http://www.cossa.org/growing_old.htm. See also Murray Gendell and Jacob S. Siegel, "Trends in Retirement Age by Sex, 1950–2005," *Monthly Labor Review* (July 1992): 22–29.

10. National Center for Health Statistics: www.cdc.gov/nchs/data/nvsr/nvar51_03.pdf.

11. National Center for Health Statistics: http://www.cdc.gov/nchs/data/statnt/statnt21.pdf.

12. William Graebner, *A History of Retirement: The Meaning and Function of an American Institution, 1885–1978* (New Haven, Yale University Press, 1980), 29.

13. For older images of retirement, see Graebner, *A History of Retirement*. See also Costa, *The Evolution of Retirement*. Costa writes, "Early twentieth-century writers on the old argued that technological change in manufacturing was forcing older men out of the labor force. Machinery was increasingly operated at such fast speeds that older workers could not keep pace and were relegated to the 'industrial scrap heap.'" (pp. 21–22).

On the change in the public image of retirement, Graebner notes, "In advertisements published in over three hundred newspapers in the late 1940's, [retirement] was the joy of being at the ballpark on a weekday afternoon" (p. 225). David J. Ekerdt and Evelyn Clark, "Selling Retirement in Financial Planning Advertisements," *Journal of Aging Studies* 15, no. 1 (March 2001): 55–71, provide a perceptive content analysis of current advertisements aimed at the retired and those planning retirement. Most of these ads hope to sell the services of investment firms. The ads picture retirees as consumers of leisure activities and convey that retirement requires financial security. For retirement as opportunity, see Betty Friedan, *The Fountain of Age* (New York: Simon and Schuster, 1993).

Changes in one man's image of his own retirement, from his teenage anticipation of a rocking chair on a porch to his very active actual retirement in his sixties, are described in Bill Bailey, "Changing Images of Retirement," *Generations* 23, no. 4 (winter 1999/2000): 42–45.

14. Eduardo Porter and Mary Williams Walsh, "Retirement Becomes a Rest Stop as Pensions and Benefits Shrink," *New York Times,* February 9, 2005, A1.

15. Retirement planning, such as it is, tends to be financial planning. It appears that no more than 40% of prospective retirees have any plans for their retirements: see Jungmeen E. Kim and Phyllis Moen, "Moving into Retirement: Preparation and Transitions in Late Midlife," in Margie E. Lachman, ed., *Handbook of Midlife Development* (New York: Wiley, 2001), 487–527, esp. 492–93. Regarding preretirement anxiety, see Orit Nuttman-Schwartz, "Like a High Wave: Adjustment to Retirement," *Gerontologist* 44, no. 2 (April 2004): 229–36. Also see Wesla L. Fletcher and Robert O. Hansson, "Assessing the Social Components of Retirement Anxiety," *Psychology and Aging* 6, no. 1 (1991): 76–85. Parents can provide both positive and negative models of retirement. Several of our respondents said that one reason they wanted to retire while they were in good health was that their parents had postponed retirement until they were infirm. In this connection, see Karyl E. MacEwen, Julian Baring, E. Kevin Kelloway, and Susan F. Higginbottam, "Predicting Retirement Anxiety: The Roles of Parental Socialization and Personal Planning," *Journal of Social Psychology* 135, no. 2 (April 1995): 203–13.

16. Maximiliane E. Szinovacz, "Contexts and Pathways: Retirement as Institution, Process, and Experience," in *Retirement: Reasons, Processes, and Results,* ed. Gary A. Adams and Terry A. Beehr (New York: Springer, 2003), 6–52, esp. 33–40.

17. Janet L. Barnes-Farrell, "Beyond Health and Wealth: Attitudinal and Other In-

fluences on Retirement Decision-Making," in *Retirement: Reasons, Processes, and Results*, ed. Gary A. Adams and Terry A. Beehr (New York: Springer, 2003) 159–87.

18. See Jungmeen E. Kim and Phyllis Moen, "Retirement Transitions, Gender, and Psychological Well-Being: A Life-Course, Ecological Model," *Journals of Gerontology, Psychological Sciences and Social Sciences* 57B, no. 3 (May 2002): 212–22.

Chapter 1. Reasons for Retirement

1. About half of a random urban sample of men and women eighteen years of age or older agreed that there was a definite age by which retirement would be expected. Most put that age between sixty and sixty-five. Richard A. Settersten Jr. and Gunhild O. Hagestad, "What's the Latest? Cultural Age Deadlines for Educational and Work Transitions," *Gerontologist* 36, no. 5 (October 1996): 602–13.

2. On the role of pensions and wealth in retirement timing, see Richard Burkhauser and Joseph Quinn, "Is Mandatory Retirement Overrated? Evidence from the 1970's," *Journal of Human Resources* 18 (summer 1983): 337–58. See also Roger Gordon and Alan Blinder, "Market Wages, Reservation Wages, and Retirement Decisions," *Journal of Public Economics* 14, no. 2 (October 1980): 277–308. Also see Laurence J. Kotlikoff and David A. Wise, "Employee Retirement and a Firm's Pension Plan," in David A. Wise, ed., *The Economics of Aging* (Chicago: University of Chicago Press, 1989), 279–330. On the effects of Social Security, see Michael Hurd and Michael Boskin, "The Effect of Social Security on Retirement in the Early 1970s," *Quarterly Journal of Economics* 99, no. 45 (November 1984): 767–90. On the importance of post-retirement health insurance, see Lynn A. Karoly and Jeannette A. Rogowski, "The Effect of Access to Post-Retirement Health Insurance on the Decision to Retire Early," *Industrial and Labor Relations Review* 48, no. 1 (October 1994): 103–23.

3. A number of studies have examined reasons for retirement. A compact review of the literature can be found in John C. Henretta, Christopher G. Chan, and Angela M. O'Rand, "Retirement Reason versus Retirement Process: Examining the Reasons for Retirement Typology," *Journal of Gerontology* 47, no. 1 (January 1992): S1–7. They report that typical studies have been surveys in which respondents were asked to choose which of a list of possible reasons for retirement was responsible for their own decision. Before mandatory retirement was outlawed, an important distinction in the lists of reasons was between having wanted to retire and having been compelled to retire. But imposed retirements continue, law or no law. Another useful summary of the literature is provided by Maximiliane E. Szinovacz and Stanley DeViney, "Marital Characteristics and Retirement Decisions," *Research on Aging* 22, no. 5 (September 2000): 470–98.

4. Reporting on men receiving Social Security retirement benefits in 1980–81, Henretta et al. ("Retirement Reason versus Retirement Process") note that in about half the cases more than one reason was given for the retirement decision. They also note that one category of reason for retirement that the study used was "wanted to retire." "Wanted to retire," of course, could mean anything from wanting to escape a conflict with a boss to wanting to move to Europe. Reporting as a finding so unspecific a reason for retirement suggests some of the problems of survey studies.

5. That family obligations foster women's retirement but not men's is noted in Robert O. Hansson, Paul D. DeKoekkoek, Wynell M. Neece, and David W. Patterson, "Successful Aging at Work: Annual Review, 1992–1996: The Older Worker and Transitions to Retirement," *Journal of Vocational Behavior* 51 (October 1997): 202–33. They write, "Men appear less likely to retire if their spouse is in poor health, reasoning that their continued employment will provide the finances necessary to ensure

proper medical care. Conversely, women appear more likely to retire if their spouse is in poor health so that they might be able to provide direct care" (p. 218). Feeling an obligation to help an ill spouse is not the only marital factor that leads women to retire; many women also feel an obligation to be with a spouse who would otherwise spend his days alone. For other reports on women's responsiveness to familial responsibilities, see Christopher Ruhm, "Gender Differences in Employment Behavior during Late Middle Age," *Journals of Gerontology, Psychological Sciences and Social Sciences* 51, no. 1 (January 1996): S11–18, and Eliza K. Pavalko and Julie E. Artis, "Women's Caregiving and Paid Work: Causal Relationships in Late Midlife," *Journals of Gerontology, Psychological Sciences and Social Sciences* 52B, no. 4 (July 1997): S170–79. On the other hand, Szinovacz and DeViney report that husbands are more likely than wives to retire because of an ill spouse, presumably because the husbands are less capable of managing a household and a job simultaneously. See Szinovacz and DeViney, "Marital Characteristics and Retirement Decisions," 490.

6. Henretta, Chan, and O'Rand, "Retirement Reason versus Retirement Process," find that "[h]aving a younger wife slows a husband's retirement and having an older wife speeds it up." They believe that if wives are not ready for retirement, their husbands are likely to postpone their own retirements. As the material here suggests, another possible scenario is that the husband goes ahead with retirement and encourages his wife to join him.

7. See Jan E. Mutchler, Jeffrey A. Burr, Michael P. Massagli, and Amy Pienta, "Work Transitions and Health in Later Life," *Journals of Gerontology, Psychological Sciences and Social Sciences* 54B, no. 5 (September 1999): S252–61.

Chapter 2. The Departure from Work

1. Jan E. Mutchler, Jeffrey A. Burr, Amy Pienta, and Michael P. Massagli, "Pathways to Labor Force Exit: Work Transitions and Work Instability," *Journals of Gerontology, Psychological Sciences and Social Sciences* 52B, no. 1 (January 1997): S4–12. Those of our respondents who described blurred boundaries between working and retirement realized, when they began cutting back on work, that they were entering retirement, though it might at first have been only a partial retirement. See also John C. Henretta, "Changing Perspectives on Retirement," *Journals of Gerontology, Psychological Sciences and Social Sciences* 52B, no. 1 (January 1997): S1–3.

2. Mutchler et al., "Pathways to Labor Force Exit."

3. People do not usually have firm retirement plans until they come close to retirement age. Ekerdt et al. report that in response to a survey question about their retirement plans, some 43% of workers in their fifties said they had not given retirement much thought or had no plans. Another 13% said they would never retire. Many of these will, of course, change their minds. It seems likely, too, that many of those who offered specific dates for their retirement were offering guesses rather than plans. See David J. Ekerdt, Jennifer Hackney, Karl Kosloski, and Stanley DeViney, "Eddies in the Stream: The Prevalence of Uncertain Plans for Retirement," *Journals of Gerontology, Psychological Sciences and Social Sciences* 56B, no. 3 (May 2001): S162–73.

4. In "Eddies in the Stream" Ekerdt et al. show that those who believe they will retire at a certain age, and so are at least launched on an orderly retirement (barring derailment by illness or occupational vicissitude), show a steady increase in the thought they give to retirement as they approach their planned retirement age.

5. Dan Jacobson, "Celebrating Good-bye: Functional Components in Farewell Parties for Retiring Employees in Israel," *Journal of Aging Studies* 10, no. 3 (fall 1996): 223–36, esp. 231.

6. Joel S. Savishinsky, using interviews and ethnographic observations, described the retirement experiences of twenty-six middle-income people in his *Breaking the Watch: The Meanings of Retirement in America* (Ithaca: Cornell University Press, 2000) and in several papers. His respondents found formal ceremonies disappointing. He writes, "The climax to years of work was anticlimactic" (Savishinsky, "The Unbearable Lightness of Retirement," *Research on Aging* 17, no. 3 [September 1995]: 243–57, esp. 246). For the range of ceremonies, see his *Breaking the Watch,* 43–57. Savishinsky believes that informal ceremonies—lunches or parties not organized by superiors in the firm—were more gratifying to his respondents because the feelings expressed were felt to be more genuine.

7. Jacobson, "Celebrating Good-bye."

Chapter 3. Gains and Losses

1. For a compact review of the literature, see Kim and Moen, "Retirement Transitions, Gender, and Psychological Well-Being," 212–22. In their study of retirees from a half dozen firms they find that retirees who had left work within the preceding two years had higher morale than not-yet-retired workers over fifty and also higher morale than retirees who had been retired more than two years. Similar findings of early positive response to retirement followed by decline were also reported by David J. Ekerdt, Raymond Bosse, and Sue Levkoff, in "An Empirical Test for Phases of Retirement: Findings from the Normative Aging Study," *Journal of Gerontology* 40, no. 1 (1985): 95–101, and by Terry L. Gall, David R. Evans, and John Howard, "The Retirement Adjustment Process: Changes in the Well-Being of Male Retirees across Time," *Journals of Gerontology, Psychological Sciences and Social Sciences* 52B, no. 3 (May 1997): 110–17. Much variation occurs among retirees, however.

2. See Gall, Evans, and Howard, "The Retirement Adjustment Process." Also see Christopher F. Sharply and Priscilla G. Yardley, "'What Makes Me Happy Now That I'm Older': A Retrospective Report of Attitudes and Strategies Used to Adjust to Retirement as Reported by Older Persons," *Applied Health Behavior* 1, no. 2 (1999): 31–35. Virginia Richardson and Keith M. Kitty, in their "Adjustment to Retirement: Continuity vs. Discontinuity," *International Journal of Aging and Human Development* 33, no. 2 (1991): 151–69, report that once people get used to being retired they pretty much maintain their level of adaptation.

3. Being pushed into retirement makes for adaptive difficulties. In addition to materials in the preceding chapters, see James W. Walker, Douglas C. Kimmel, and Karl F. Price, "Retirement Style and Retirement Satisfaction: Retirees Aren't All Alike," *International Journal of Aging and Human Development* 12, no. 4 (1980–81): 267–81.

On the basis of a small sample study, Gail A. Hornstein and Seymour Wapner classified retirees by the way in which they treated the retirement experience. They proposed four orientations. In what they call "Transition to Old Age," retirees "settle into a quiet and circumscribed existence" and are pleased to be retired. In what they call "New Beginning," retirement is seen by retirees to offer them opportunity for a new life, and again retirees are pleased to be retired. In what Hornstein and Wapner call "Continuation," retirees essentially go on doing what they had been doing before their retirement—some academics continue doing research, for example—and for them retirement does not matter much one way or the other. Finally, in what Hornstein and Wapner call "Imposed Disruption," retirees lose satisfactions that came with their work, and are thereafter persistently unhappy. See Hornstein and Wapner, "Modes of Experiencing and Adapting to Retirement," *International Journal of Aging and Human Development* 21, no. 4 (1985): 291–315.

4. Michael Young and Tom Shuller consider loss of structure to be among the most unsettling aspects of ending work. See Young and Shuller, *Life After Work: The Arrival of the Ageless Society* (London: HarperCollins, 1991). Hornstein and Wapner report that in the absence of work all the respondents in their small sample, irrespective of their happiness or unhappiness in retirement, had to develop an internal sense of structure that would replace the external structure that work had provided. They speculate that the energy that new retirees sometimes put into getting their files or attics or garages in order can be seen as a response to a sense of internal disarray. Hornstein and Wapner, "Modes of Experiencing and Adapting to Retirement."

5. Mihalyi Csikszentmihalyi, *Flow: The Psychology of Optimal Experience* (New York: Harper & Row, 1990).

6. A comparison of retired members of a health maintenance organization with members who were still employed found that the retired reported significantly lower levels of stress. Lorraine T. Midanik, Krikor Soghikian, Laura J. Ransom, and Irene S. Tekawa, "The Effect of Retirement on Mental Health and Health Behaviors: The Kaiser Permanente Retirement Study," *Journals of Gerontology, Psychological Sciences and Social Sciences* 50B, no. 1 (January 1995): S59–61.

Chapter 4. Money

1. Our respondents were more knowledgeable than the general population. Ekerdt and Hackney report that about a fifth of those soon to retire who can expect some sort of pension benefits, when asked what those benefits will be, say that they do not know. David J. Ekerdt and Jennifer Kay Hackney, "Workers' Ignorance of Retirement Benefits," *The Gerontologist* 42, no. 4 (August 2002): 533–51, esp. table 2, "Percentage of Workers with 'Don't Know' Responses by Temporal Proximity to Benefit Receipt or Retirement."

2. A study in the mid-1980s found that on average the after-tax household income of married couples dropped by 22 percent after the retirement of the household head. Rose M. Rubin and Michael L. Nieswiadomy, "Economic Adjustments of Households on Entry into Retirement," *Journal of Applied Gerontology* 14, no. 4 (December 1995): 467–82.

3. Linda K. George, "Economic Status and Subjective Well-Being: A Review of the Literature and an Agenda for Future Research," in *Aging, Money, and Life Satisfaction: Aspects of Financial Gerontology,* ed. Neal E. Cutler, Davis W. Gregg, and M. Powell Lawton (New York: Springer, 1992), 69–99.

4. Douglas Fore reports that there is substantial evidence that financial planning is difficult and often neglected. He notes a finding that in a ten-year interval about half of those who participated in the academically oriented TIAA-CREF programs simply kept their initial arrangement in force. See Douglas Fore, "Do We Have a Retirement Crisis in America?" *TIAA-CREF Research Dialogue,* no. 77 (September 2003): 1–18. esp. 3.

5. Apprehension regarding retirement income is common among the soon-to-retire. There is more than adequate justification for this apprehension among those without private pensions who will look to Social Security for the bulk—or the entirety—of their retirement income. Some will find that their payments have been diminished by spells in which they were without employment and by low wages when they did have employment. Groups especially likely to be in this fix are minorities and women. In the past few years there has been very active debate among those responsible for national policy and among commentators from all parts of the political spectrum regarding the future of Social Security. For a discussion of issues I found useful, see the report made to the Senate Committee on Aging by David M. Walker, Comptroller General, U.S.

General Accounting Office, and Barbara D. Bovbjerg, Director, Education, Workforce, and Income Security Issues, U.S. General Accounting Office. I also found useful the appended prepared statement by Senator Russ Feingold. They were published as Senate hearing 108-1, "Analyzing Social Security: GAO Weighs the President's Commission's Proposals, January 15, 2003," by the U.S. Government Printing Office, as the first of Special Committee on Aging Committee Hearings, 108th Congress, and are available both from the Superintendent of Documents, U.S. Government Printing Office, Congressional Sales Office, and on the Internet at http://www.access.gpo.gov/congress/senate/senate22sh108.html.

6. This observation makes me skeptical of the value of private retirement accounts as an alternative to Social Security. It seems to me that it will be those who had smaller incomes when they worked, and in consequence smaller pensions, who will have the least experience with investing and be the most vulnerable to mistakes.

7. Linda K. George writes, "There is consistent evidence that older adults are more satisfied with their financial resources than younger and middle-aged adults. . . . There is no evidence from the limited longitudinal data bases available that financial satisfaction declines with age or time since retirement. . . . This pattern . . . contrasts with that for financial resources. . . . [L]ongitudinal studies consistently indicate that income (and perhaps other financial assets) decline during later life." She also notes that "Older adults are . . . satisfied with substantially lower levels of income than younger adults, even after adjustments for family size." See George, "Economic Status and Subjective Well-Being."

8. Families headed by someone sixty-five or older appear to require only 65 percent to 80 percent of their preretirement income to maintain their living standard after retirement. Michael Alan Stoller and Eleanor Palo Stoller, "Perceived Income Adequacy among Elderly Retirees," *Journal of Applied Gerontology* 22, no. 2 (June 2003): 236–51, quoting a 1996 seminar presentation by F. Thomas Juster, Beth Soldo, Raynard Kington, and Olivia Mitchell, available as *Aging Well: Health, Wealth, and Retirement* (Washington, D.C.: Consortium of Social Science Associations).

9. George, "Economic Status and Subjective Well-Being."

10. Richard W. Johnson and Rudolph G. Penner report that older Americans are spending an ever-larger proportion of their incomes on health care and that this trend can be expected to continue. They think spending on health care will make saving for retirement more difficult and pose severe problems for some among the already retired. Retirees' health care expenses, despite Medicare coverage, can include Medicare premiums, premiums for supplemental Medigap insurance, and direct payments to health care providers to pay for Medicare deductibles, co-payments, and uncovered services. See Johnson and Penner, "Will Health Care Costs Erode Retirement Security?" An Issue in Brief from the Center for Retirement Research at Boston College, No. 23, October 2004, available through the website http://www.bc.edu/crr.

Lori Achman and Marsha Gold of Mathematica Policy Research have found that Medicare enrollees who elected the Medicare managed care option paid nearly fifty percent more in out-of-pocket costs for their health care in 2001 than they did in 1999. Those in the poorest health experienced the highest rate of growth in out-of-pocket costs. Achman and Gold report that in 2001 HMO enrollees in poor health spent about three times as much as those in good health, with average annual costs of, respectively, $3,578 and $1,195. See their "Out-of-pocket Health Care Expenses for Medicare HMO Beneficiaries: Estimates by Health Status, 1999–2001," Washington, D.C., Mathematica Policy Research, Inc., The Commonwealth Fund, February 2002. The publication is available online at http://www.cmwf.org/publications/publications_show.htm?doc_id=221297.

11. At 3% inflation, money loses half its value in twenty-four years. An income that is just good enough when the retiree is sixty-five will be inadequate should the retiree reach eighty-nine. At 6% inflation, money loses half its value in twelve years. Retirees are among the big losers when inflation hits a currency.

12. Fore, "Do We Have a Retirement Crisis in America?" pp. 1–18. Statistics for the article were provided by the Employee Benefit Research Institute of Washington, D.C., and have as their source publications of the Social Security Administration.

In 2003 just under half of those employed in private industry were covered by a retirement plan provided by their employers. Defined benefit plans, which promise a specific income in retirement, have for some time been giving way to defined contribution plans in which income in retirement is dependent on the amount the employee has invested. *Monthly Labor Review* 126, no. 10 (October 2003): 2. Defined contribution plans require the eventual retiree to shoulder the risk that his or her investments will not work out.

13. Fore, "Do We Have a Retirement Crisis in America?" p. 6.

14. Ibid., p. 8.

15. Robert C. Atchley, in a paper making projections for the immediate future, writes: "Current trends suggest a shaky future for retirement income for all but the corporate and government elite that have both high incomes and generous defined benefit pensions. However, we should not expect the public to stand idly by and do nothing to alter this scenario. When retirement income problems become a reality for large segments of the older population, we should expect increased intergenerational political support for public policy proposals that improve income security. The sooner we come to understand and accept that a strong Social Security system, widely available employer pensions, and tax incentives for retirement savings all play a vital role in later life income security, the greater the likelihood that we can avoid large numbers of elders who have to endure the indignity of poverty." See his "Retirement Income Security: Past, Present, and Future," *Generations* 21, no. 2 (summer 1997): 9–13, esp. 13.

Chapter 5. Social Isolation

1. A small study of couples who had moved to New England from at least two states' distance found similar reports of social isolation among stay-at-home wives despite good marriages and, sometimes, concerned husbands. See Robert S. Weiss, "The Provisions of Social Relationships," in Zick Rubin, ed., *Doing Unto Others: Joining, Molding, Conforming, Helping, Loving* (Englewood Cliffs, N.J.: Prentice-Hall, 1974), 17–26.

2. The distinction in the text is between a relationship with a life partner, whose absence makes for vulnerability to loneliness, and membership in a social community, whose absence makes for vulnerability to the experience of social isolation. For further discussion of the distinction see my *Loneliness: The Experience of Emotional and Social Isolation* (Cambridge, Mass.: MIT Press, 1974) and "A Taxonomy of Relationships," *Journal of Personal and Social Relationships* 15, no. 5 (October 1998): 671–84. For explorations of the usefulness of the distinction see Elizabeth Dugan and Vira R. Kivett, "The Importance of Emotional and Social Isolation to Loneliness among Very Old Adults," *Gerontologist* 34, no. 3 (June 1994): 340–46 and Berna van Baarsen, Tom A. B. Snijders, Johannes H. Smit, and Marijte A. J. Van Duijn, "Lonely but Not Alone: Emotional Isolation and Social Isolation as Two Distinct Dimensions of Loneliness in Older People," *Educational and Psychological Measurement* 61, no. 1 (February 2001): 119–35.

3. A demonstration that social isolation contributes to depression is in Janet M.

Wilmoth and Pei-chun Chen, "Immigrant Status, Living Arrangements, and Depressive Symptoms among Middle-Aged and Older Adults," *Journals of Gerontology, Psychological Sciences and Social Sciences* 58B, no. 5 (September 2003): S305–13. Depression can, of course, cause people to withdraw and so foster social isolation, just as social isolation can foster depression. For one effort to disentangle the causal relationship between depression and social isolation, see Peter A. Barnett and Ian H. Gotlib, "Psychosocial Functioning and Depression: Distinguishing among Antecedents, Concomitants, and Consequences," *Psychological Bulletin* 104, no. 1 (July 1988): 97–116.

4. A carefully controlled study of residents of a nursing home found that every increase in the level of "social engagement" predicted an increase in longevity. "Social engagement" meant not only friendly interaction and participation in group activities but also indirect engagement with the social world through reading and keeping one's personal space presentable. Dan K. Kiely and Jonathan M. Flacker, "The Protective Effect of Social Engagement on 1-Year Mortality in a Long-Stay Nursing Home Population," *Journal of Clinical Epidemiology* 56, no. 5 (May 2003): 472–78. For a discussion of pathways that might link social integration and well-being, see Sheldon Cohen and Ian Brissette, "Social Integration and Health: The Case of the Common Cold," *Journal of Social Structure* 1, no. 3, online at: http://www.cmu.edu/joss/content/articles/volume1/.

5. James House, "Social Isolation Kills, but How and Why?" *Psychosomatic Medicine* 63, no. 2 (March/April 2001): 273–74.

Chapter 6. Using the Time of Retirement

1. Moen et al. have found that those who maintain a mix of activities report higher levels of well-being. See Phyllis Moen, Vivian Fields, Heather E. Quick, and Heather Hofmeister, "A Life-Course Approach to Retirement and Social Integration," in Karl Pillemer, Phyllis Moen, Elaine Wethington, and Nina Glasgow, eds., *Social Integration in the Second Half of Life* (Baltimore: Johns Hopkins University Press, 2002), 100.

2. David Ekerdt, "The Busy Ethic: Moral Continuity between Work and Retirement," *The Gerontologist* 26, no. 3 (June 1986): 239–44.

3. Other investigators have found a gender split in the value placed on pure sociability, with men giving relatively more value to continuing to make a difference in the world rather than having an opportunity to gain the company of others. Aspects of the gender difference are described by Linda K. George, Gerda G. Fillenbaum, and Erdman B. Palmore, "Sex Differences in the Antecedents and Consequences of Retirement," *Journal of Gerontology* 39, no. 3 (May 1984): 364–71. See also Kim Perren, Sara Arber, and Kate Davidson, "Men's Organizational Affiliations in Later Life: The Influence of Social Class and Marital Status on Informal Group Membership," *Ageing and Society* 23 (2003): 69–82.

4. This is unusual in the United States except among the self-employed but has been shown in Sweden to be both practical and popular in a range of occupations. See Sara E. Rix, *Older Workers* (Santa Barbara, Calif.: ABC-CLIO, 1990), 108, 116–19.

5. Economists tend to characterize as a bridge job any work that follows career employment and precedes what they would consider full retirement. See Peter B. Doeringer, "Economic Security, Labor Market Flexibility, and Bridges to Retirement," in Peter B. Doeringer, ed., *Bridges to Retirement* (Ithaca: Cornell University Press, 1990), 3–19, esp. 4. See also Christopher J. Ruhm, "Bridge Jobs and Partial Retirement," *Journal of Labor Economics* 8, no. 4 (1990): 482–501, and Christopher J. Ruhm, "Career Jobs, Bridge Employment, and Retirement," in Doeringer, *Bridges to Retirement*, 92–107. A distinction between a bridge job and work as a retirement activity is that

the former is a tapering off of employment, the latter just one option for the use of the time freed by the ending of career work.

Diane E. Herz, in "Work after Early Retirement: An Increasing Trend among Men," *Monthly Labor Review* 118, no. 4 (April 1995): 13–21, suggests that some early retirees seek continued work because they were pushed into retirement and were not yet willing to accept themselves as genuinely retired.

6. Recently retired managers and professionals who had found work or were looking for work are discussed in David A. Karp, "The Social Construction of Retirement among Professionals," *The Gerontologist* 29 (1989): 750–60.

7. Francis G. Caro and Scott A. Bass, "Receptivity to Volunteering in the Immediate Postretirement Period," *Journal of Applied Gerontology* 16, no. 4 (December 1997): 427–41. See also Jan E. Mutchler, Jeffrey A. Burr, and Francis G. Caro, "From Paid Worker to Volunteer: Leaving the Paid Workforce and Volunteering in Later Life," *Social Forces* 81, no. 4 (June 2003): 1267–93.

8. Susan M. Chambre, "Volunteering: A Substitute for Role Loss in Old Age? An Empirical Test of Activity Theory," *The Gerontologist* 24, no. 3 (1984): 292–98.

9. On the basis of a 1999 national sample survey for the organization Independent Sector, it appears that almost a quarter of Americans over the age of sixty-five report themselves as having served as volunteers for a religious institution at least once during the preceding year, almost a tenth as having served as volunteers at least once for an educational institution, and almost a tenth as having served as volunteers at least once for a health organization. The amount of time given to volunteering among those who volunteer at all seems, on average, to be between three and four hours per week. However, activities considered in arriving at that estimate included informal help to neighbors. See Susan Saxon-Harrold, Michael McCormack, and Keith Hume, "America's Senior Volunteers," available online at http://www.IndependentSector.org. Retirees who do volunteer work generally donate more time than do people still employed. Phyllis Moen, William A. Erickson, Madhurima Agarwal, Vivian Fields, and Laurie Todd, *Final Report of the Cornell Retirement and Well-Being Study*, Bronfenbrenner Life Course Center, Cornell University, 2000, as reported by Mutchler, Burr, and Caro, "From Paid Worker to Volunteer."

10. Just about any level of part-time volunteering for a single organization, so long as it is not full-time, seems to have physical benefits (indicated by reduced risk of mortality). But forty or more hours per week of volunteering or volunteering for more than one organization seems to dissipate its benefits. See Mark Musick, A. Regula Herzog, and James House, "Volunteering and Mortality among Older Adults: Findings from a National Sample," *The Journals of Gerontology, Series B: Psychological Sciences and Social Sciences* 54B, no. 3 (1999): S173–80. Explaining the beneficial consequences of reasonable levels of volunteering remains a matter of surmise. One assessment is that "Volunteering improves health, but it is also most likely that healthier people are more likely to volunteer. Good health is preserved by volunteering; it keeps healthy volunteers healthy." John Wilson, "Volunteering," *Annual Review of Sociology*, 2000, 215–51.

Mutchler, Burr, and Caro report research that identifies other benefits of volunteering in addition to improved health: enhanced life satisfaction, improved self-esteem, and improved psychological well-being. See Mutchler, Burr, and Caro, "From Paid Worker to Volunteer."

11. There have been few published studies of retired people's motivations for participating in voluntary associations. One, of motives for participating in a Learning in Retirement program that offered college-level work for the elderly, found a combination of desire to learn (the focus of the group) and desire for social contact. One might

, expect to find this combination, perhaps with different levels of the two components, accounting for participation in other voluntary associations as well. See Ahjin Kim and Sharan B. Merriam, "Motivations for Learning among Older Adults in a Learning in Retirement Institute," *Educational Gerontology* 30, no. 4 (2004): 441–45.

12. That hobbies contribute to life satisfaction has been found by studies of retired physicians and retired civil servants. See Mary Guerriero Austrom, Anthony J. Perkins, Teresa M. Damush, and Hugh C. Hendrie, "Predictors of Life Satisfaction in Retired Physicians and Spouses," *Social Psychiatry and Psychiatric Epidemiology* 38, no. 3 (March 2003): 134–41, and Saraswati Mishra, "Leisure Activities and Life Satisfaction in Old Age: A Case Study of Retired Government Employees Living in Urban Areas," *Activities, Adaptation and Aging* 16, no. 4 (1992): 7–26.

13. Csikszentmihalyi, *Flow.*

14. See Savishinsky, *Breaking the Watch,* 51–53, 56.

15. Naomi Rosh White and Peter B. White, "Travel as Transition: Identity and Place," *Annals of Tourism Research* 31, no. 1 (January 2004): 200–218.

16. This is discussed, along with other contributions of travel, by William L. Obenour, "Understanding the Meaning of the 'Journey' to Budget Travelers," *International Journal of Tourism Research* 6 (2004): 1–15. Not all budget travelers are young. And budget travel is not so different in its aims, gratification, and meanings from any other kind of travel.

17. This is not to minimize the importance of seeing the sights. A traveler is likely to use "must see" attractions like the Statue of Liberty to organize time at a destination. Failure to see a must-see attraction can mean a flawed trip. Imagine having been to Cairo without seeing the pyramids. See, in this connection, D. MacCannell, *The Tourist: A New Theory of the Leisure Class* (New York: Schocken Books, 1976).

18. Ekerdt, "The Busy Ethic."

Chapter 7. Marriage and Family

1. For a discussion of the ways in which differences in men's lives and in women's lives fan out as the men and women grow older, see Mark D. Hayward and Mei-Chun Liu, "Men and Women in Their Retirement Years: A Demographic Profile," in Maximiliane Szinovacz, David Ekerdt, and Barbara Vinick, eds., *Families and Retirement* (Newbury Park, Calif.: Sage, 1992), 23–50.

2. Japanese women whose husbands are retired from all-absorbing careers sometimes refer to the men's increased presence as a nuisance. One author reports: "The language used to describe the hapless homebound and dependent retired male says it all: . . . big bag of garbage or wet fallen leaves, clinging and sticky." Merry Isaacs White, *Perfectly Japanese: Making Families in an Era of Upheaval* (Berkeley: University of California Press, 2002), 63–96. The quotation appears on p. 94.

3. Research suggests that retirement's increased togetherness does indeed require adaptation on the part of husband and wife, but the adaptation generally is made rather easily; in addition, the togetherness has compensations. The partner who has become accustomed to sole occupancy of the home during the day—usually, but not always, the wife—can complain that the other partner's retirement has resulted in an impingement on space, an invasion of privacy, and a disruption of routine, but most couples find that these negatives are outweighed by the increased companionship. In general, as people move into their seventies and eighties they report greater marital satisfaction. For a review of these issues, see Robert C. Atchley, "Retirement and Marital Satisfaction," in Szinovacz, Ekerdt, and Vinick, *Families and Retirement*, 145–58. See also Barbara H. Vinick and David J. Ekerdt, "Retirement: What Happens to Hus-

band-Wife Relationships?" in *Journal of Geriatric Psychiatry* 24, no. 1 (1991): 23–40, esp. 26–27.

4. On the basis of a study of ninety-two couples in which the husband retired, Vinick and Ekerdt report that over half their female informants had experienced some intrusion of the husband into the wife's sphere of activity. Almost always, though, the wives thought of the intrusions as minor nuisances or annoyances rather than significant problems. See Vinick and Ekerdt, "Retirement: What Happens to Husband-Wife Relationships?"

5. Phyllis Moen, Jungmeen E. Kim, and Heather Hofmeister, "Couples' Work/Retirement Transitions, Gender, and Marital Quality," *Social Psychology Quarterly* 64, no. 1 (2001): 55–71.

6. Vinick and Ekerdt were told by half of the wives in their study that they themselves felt more at ease now that their husbands were freed from the tyranny of the job. They believed their husbands were now calmer, more patient, and more serene. Vinick and Ekerdt, "Retirement: What Happens to Husband-Wife Relationships?"

7. Satisfaction with their marriages has been shown to contribute to satisfaction with retirement among both husbands and wives. But the ability to negotiate marital disputes with equanimity—quite apart from satisfaction with the marriage—seems to be important to husbands as a determinant of satisfaction with retirement, but not to wives. See Cenita Kupperbusch, Robert W. Levenson, and Rachel Ebling, "Predicting Husbands' and Wives' Retirement Satisfaction from the Emotional Qualities of Marital Interaction," *Journal of Social and Personal Relationships* 20, no. 3 (June 2003): 335–54.

8. The division of household work in retirement may be somewhat less traditional than it was earlier in the marriage, but even after retirement husbands continue to be more likely to do "men's work," wives to do "women's work." Most important for marital satisfaction may be the conviction that the work of maintaining the home has been shared fairly. See Lorraine T. Dorfman, "Couples in Retirement: Division of Household Work," in Szinovacz, Ekerdt, and Vinick, *Families and Retirement,* 159–73. Dorfman provides a useful review of the literature on household division of labor among retired couples.

9. Vinick and Ekerdt write, "We were impressed by the caretaking responsibilities assumed by retired children." Many of their respondents helped aged parents with shopping, cleaning, and transportation. Their respondents' retirement also made it easier for the respondents to take time just to visit the parents. Vinick and Ekerdt, "Retirement: What Happens to Husband-Wife Relationships?"

Index

Names of respondents are included in a separate index following the main index.